schoolmasters
of the tenth century

schoolmasters
of the tenth century

CORA E. LUTZ

ARCHON BOOKS   1977

Library of Congress Cataloging in Publication Data

Lutz, Cora Elizabeth
   Schoolmasters of the tenth century.

   Bibliography: p.
   Includes index.
   1. Teachers—Europe—Biography. 2. Education, Medieval. I.
Title.
LA2371.L87   371.1'0092'2   [B]   76-29644
ISBN 0-208-01628-7

© Cora E. Lutz 1977

First printed 1977 as an Archon Book
an imprint of The Shoe String Press Inc
Hamden, Connecticut 06514

Printed in the United States of America

To the memory of
George Lincoln Hendrickson

Contents

Illustrations

Preface

Two MEDIEVAL SCHOLARS of great distinction as teachers were Remigius of Auxerre, "doctor egregius," in the ninth century, and Fulbert of Chartres, "Socrates noster," in the eleventh. In the intervening troubled century, the chain of scholars who were responsible for preserving learning and passing it from ancient times to modern continued unbroken. Most of these scholars were schoolmasters, the pupils of Remigius and their pupils, until one of them became the teacher of Fulbert. These are the men with whom this study is concerned.

An effective method of portraying these schoolmasters of the tenth century would be to present them playing their roles upon a circular stage which slowly revolves as the century progresses. Against a cyclorama depicting the historical events of the time, all the actors would be on the stage at once, making their entrances and their exits at the appropriate times, but interacting with their fellows who are on center stage at the same time they are. Lacking such elaborate stage machinery, one can only focus the spotlight upon one actor at a time. This, of course, risks giving several erroneous impressions, first that each is alone and then that they form an orderly succession, one after the other, leaving the stage promptly with the coming of the millenium. Other factors also make it impossible to give wholly accurate and complete portrayals of these teachers. The contemporary sources of information vary greatly in length and in comprehensiveness, but chiefly in intent. In addition to the writings of the teachers themselves, they consist of biographies, chronicles of abbeys, and annals of cities. They record the activities of these men, not because they were schoolmasters, but because they led saintly lives, or were wise abbots, or astute counselors of kings. Furthermore, the biographers in particular left portraits, not photographs, of their subjects; they painted their heroes as they idealized them and as they wished to have them remembered by future generations.

An even more serious problem arises from the fact that, in considering these tenth-century schoolmasters almost entirely from the point of view of their function in society as teachers, inevitably a distorted impression is given of their total contribution to their age.

Although restricted by these disadvantages, I shall try to give as complete a picture as possible of these men in their roles as teachers. I shall use the words of the masters themselves where they are available and, failing that, shall report the accounts of their pupils and associates. Following these contemporary sources I shall accept their evaluations of the effectiveness of the masters' teaching and not attempt to judge them by modern standards. But I shall try to avoid the hazard of patronizing them either by suggesting that they are interesting because they have a certain charm of provincialism, or, at the other extreme, by implying that they deserve attention because some of their ideas are "modern." My purpose is simply to show what kind of men these schoolmasters were, what education they were given and what they achieved for themselves, the subjects they taught and the methods they used to communicate them, their interpretation of their vocation for teaching, their philosophy of education, their relationship to their pupils, their success as measured by the inspiration of their teaching, and their legacy to their successors.

Modern scholars have produced excellent studies on the lives and achievements of many of these tenth-century men. I am greatly indebted to these, but, in general, I have not quoted from them because I wished to present the testimony of contemporary writers whenever possible. I have, however, used a number of the modern translations of the early sources since they have become standard. In particular, I wish to thank Harriet P. Lattin and the Columbia University Press for their kind permission to quote passages from the letters of Gerbert.

This study was given initial impetus by a fellowship from the Bollingen Foundation. I have enjoyed the advantages of carrying on my research in several of the great libraries. I am especially grateful to the staff of Sterling Memorial Library of Yale University for the innumerable courtesies extended to me. I also wish to express my gratitude to the British Library, the Bodleian Library, and the Stiftsbibliothek of St. Gall for their generous help. I am pleased to acknowledge with thanks the kind permission to reproduce miniatures from manuscripts in the Bodleian Library, the Library of St. John's College, Oxford, the British Library, the Niedersächsisches Hauptstaatsarchiv, Hanover, and the Oesterreichische Nationalbibliothek, Vienna. For allowing me to reproduce illustrations of statues and art objects, I wish to thank the Musée Curtius, Liège, the Art Institute of Chicago, the Domschatzkammer of Aachen, and the Church of St. Wolfgang at Abersee.

New Haven   C. E. L.

schoolmasters
of the tenth century

1. *St. Dunstan prostrate before Christ as Divine Wisdom*

1

The Reign of the Schoolmasters

THE TENTH CENTURY has commonly been treated as a separate entity somewhat detached from the continuity of history, comparable to a bad nightmare from which Europe awoke shortly after the millenium. The sharp strictures made by the sixteenth-century Church historian, Baronius, who quoted the Italian humanist, Lorenzo Valla, who in turn looked back to the judgment of Petrarch, when he said that the tenth century was an age of iron for its harshness, an age of lead for its evil, and an era of gloom for its intellectual sterility and ignorance,[1] long dominated the general attitude toward that period. In the last fifty years, however, the thesis that the tenth century cannot be separated from the mainstream of civilization has been successfully debated; further, the evil reputation of the age as "the nadir of the human intellect"[2] has been disputed so effectively by an examination of its cultural manifestations[3] that one even hears of a "renaissance" of the tenth century.[4]

In spite of these successful efforts to rehabilitate the age, one must concede that it was isolated culturally and did exhibit characteristics peculiar to itself. Bound by a past of invasions, wars, the destruction of all the centers of civilization, and, worse, the consequent demoralization and spiritual poverty, and threatened by a future of uncertainty with the awesome prospect of the portentous year 1000, the century yet showed remarkable powers of recuperation and surprising vitality in adjusting to unusually difficult circumstances. The most conspicuous demonstration of

3

this will to survive was the emergence of men who sought first by study to retrieve their intellectual heritage and then, by teaching, to pass it on to their heirs. To dramatize the phenomenal role of these teachers during the tenth century, one scholar has labelled the era, "le règne des maîtres d'écoles."[5]

These teachers range from Gregory, reputed to have been the son of King Edward the Elder, who left his native England to go to teach in a remote Alpine monastery at Einsiedeln, to the brilliant Gerbert who made himself the best educated man in Europe and shared his learning with hundreds, from the humblest choirboy to the young Emperor Otto III, "the wonder of the world." Although the original lack of records or their subsequent loss has left many of these men completely forgotten, and testimony to the achievements of scores of other able teachers consists of only brief references, fortunately for many of them contemporary accounts are sufficiently extensive to furnish adequate biographies. They taught in restored cathedral schools, in reformed monastery cloisters, and in countless smaller religious houses located throughout the lands of northern Europe. In England the principal centers of learning were Canterbury, Glastonbury, Winchester, York, and Ramsey; in France they were Rheims, Cluny, Laon, Tours, Fleury, Metz, Verdun, and Paris; in the Low Countries Lobbes, Ghent, Utrecht, and Liège were pre-eminent; in Germany there were schools at Aachen, Cologne, Trier, Magdeburg, Speyer, Mainz, Regensburg, Würzburg, Gandersheim, and Hildesheim; and in Switzerland three schools were famous: St. Gall, Reichenau, and Einsiedeln.

Out of the many, many schoolmasters of the tenth century who devoted their talents to the task of restoring learning, I shall concentrate on only ten—in England, Aelfric and Byrhtferth; in France, Abbo and Gerbert; in the Low Countries, Notger and Heriger; in Germany, Bruno, Bernward, and Wolfgang; and in Switzerland, Notker Labeo. To give some impression of the antecedents that made their work possible, I shall consider first two reformer-teachers, Odo and Everaclus, who were responsible for creating a milieu receptive to learning, then three monastic bishops, Dunstan, Ethelwold, and Oswald, who established schools in England.

Despite the wide variation in national origin, cultural background, native endowment, and educational experience among all these teachers and countless others of whose activities only scanty references remain, it does seem possible to draw a composite sketch of the tenth-century schoolmaster, even while always recognizing the existence of exceptions to the generalities. First of all, one must take into account the intellectual climate in which these men were living. Perhaps this can best be understood by contrasting it with the prevailing atmosphere affecting men of letters of the century that preceded it and also with that of the one that followed. The ninth century experienced what has often been called the Carolingian Renaissance, an intellectual upsurge that produced notable works of literature and advances in scholarship. The men of learning, as a result, seemed to feel great self-confidence; for example, the literati in Charlemagne's court circle regularly addressed one another as "Homer," "Horace," and "Virgil," and other famous poets of antiquity. Although they had all received their education in Church schools, they exhibited remarkable independence from them. So the philosoper-theologian, John the Scot, wrote, "No one may enter heaven except through philosophy,"[6] and the textual critic, Lupus of Ferrières, said, "Knowledge, to my mind, is its own end and goal."[7] These men were unquestionably unusual, but they tended to overestimate their own accomplishments.

Then if one looks at the eleventh century, one sees even greater manifestations of self-assurance and arrogance among the educated. The grammarian, Vilgardus, for example, was especially conceited and smug about his knowledge of the classics. It is related that one night three demons in the guise of Virgil, Horace, and Juvenal appeared to him and thanked him for what he had done for them, and, in turn, they promised him immortality.[8] Another pedant, Gerard of Sève, boasted that the German city of Bamberg was superior to Athens.[9]

The tenth century, by contrast, after the long agony of wars and invasions, provided no grounds to scholars for vainglory or excessive pride. So the schoolmasters, for the most part, were humble in their bearing. They were simple in the sense of being single-minded in their efforts to gain knowledge themselves and to renew learning in their communities. Against great odds they were attempting to restore what had been destroyed and to give the new generation what they had been able to acquire only with the greatest difficulties. To describe their efforts to gain knowledge from all good sources they often used the simile of the bees gathering honey drop by drop,[10] and one of them called learning "purest nectar." Though they recognized all too painfully their own inadequacies and limitations, they were not apologetic or self-pitying, but with great dignity they presented the best they had. Theirs was a true humility which made them willing to do almost anything to find instruction—even to become elementary pupils in classes for children taught by nuns. John of Gorze, for example, though older than his fellow-pupils, and already a priest, studied in the elementary classes taught by nuns in Metz.[11] At St. Gall, Ulric, who later became bishop of Augsburg and one of the "three brilliant stars" of his land, as a young student used to slip away when the other boys were enjoying a period of recreation and go to the wise old recluse, Wiborada, to be instructed in theology.[12] But one must never consider these men simple-minded, holy innocents, or God's fools. Indeed, one of their standard admonitions to their own students, potential teachers, was the Biblical injunction, "Be ye wise as serpents, harmless as doves." Aimoin, the devoted pupil of Abbo, in his biography of his master, testifies that in Abbo there was "columbina simplicitas" joined to "serpentina astutia."[13]

To a large extent the schoolmasters were self-taught. They demonstrated great hunger and thirst for knowledge, a metaphor which they often used.[14] Bruno, even though he was the brother of the Emperor Otto, followed the regimen of an ordinary monk and from his student days exhibited greater zeal for learning than his fellows, setting an example for industry and diligence throughout his life. To acquire a mastery of the seven liberal arts, these men as young students first learned the elements at school, then explored all the texts available in their own libraries, and after that went to other communities to receive what training they lacked. So Abbo, after his early education at Fleury, taught himself geometry and rhetoric from the books at the abbey, but went to Paris and Rheims for instruction in astronomy, and to Orléans to learn music. Gerbert went from Aurillac to Spain to study the sciences of the quadrivium and to Rheims to prepare himself in dialectic. Long after he had become the greatest scholar in Europe, he spoke of still thirsting for knowledge, and he was constantly sending to communities all over Europe searching out texts, asking to have books copied for him.

Even when hampered by the lack of texts, as they usually were, and when confronted by lazy, indifferent, or stupid pupils, a not uncommon situation, the teachers remained dedicated to their work and preferred it to all else. Wolfgang, for instance, once declined a bishopric that was offered to him by the archbishop of Cologne, and instead retired to the secluded monastery of St. Mary of Einsiedeln in the Alps to pursue his true vocation, teaching. These schoolmasters seem to have possessed the patience requisite for the task of inculcating knowledge in the completely untutored. Everaclus, for example, declared that he was willing to go over a difficult passage of a text a hundred times if necessary in order to make his pupils understand it.[15] Byrhtferth of Ramsey, trying to teach his reluctant pupils arithmetic, speaks in metaphorical language, saying that he had to apply a large poultice to cure them of dice-playing and make them receptive to his subject.[16] Notker Labeo felt obliged to make a strong defence of his method to his bishop when he took the extraordinary measure of translating fundamental texts from Latin into German for his pupils.[17] Others, like Notger of Liège and Bruno of Cologne, because of their great love of teaching, still found opportunities to instruct classes after they had assumed the demanding responsibilities of administering a diocese. Where text-books were lacking, the teachers wrote their own. In England Aelfric wrote an English-Latin grammar which emphasized a vocabulary and exercises germane to the pupils' experiences. Egbert of Liège wrote a text-book which he called *Fecunda ratis*, the "Heavily laden Ship," for his school. It consists of a series of texts of graduated difficulty to train children in reading Latin, at the same time providing interesting subjects and wholesome and edifying thoughts for young minds.[18] Frequently the teacher served also as librarian, collecting and preserving the books. His duties must often have included supervising the scriptorium and the copyists. Bernward of Hildesheim, famous for his beautiful craftsmanship in gold and silver, also most highly skilled in illuminating manuscripts, taught the art to his young monks.[19] Dunstan, in the midst of his duties as bishop, spent time in the scriptorium correcting the work of his students.[20]

These tenth-century schoolmasters, many of whom were Benedictine monks, thought of all knowledge as within the framework of the Christian experience. They followed the intention stated in the prologue to the Rule of St. Benedict where it speaks of a school as "of God's service." Although they were often taught by means of a study of the classical authors, the arts of the trivium were considered propaedeutic to a study of the Scriptures and Christian theology, and necessary for the proper performance of the Church liturgy. Few would be so extreme as to regard the poems of Virgil as dangerous, like a beautiful vase full of poisonous snakes, as Odo of Cluny dreamed of it,[21] yet all thought of the classics chiefly as ancillary to training for the use in the service of the Church, to the glory of God. Hroswitha, for example, that learned nun of Gandersheim, composed comedies in the manner of Terence to train her pupils in dramatic poetry without exposing them to the indelicacies of the Roman playwright. Even the old standard encyclopedia of the liberal arts, the *De Nuptiis Mercurii et Philologiae* of Martianus Capella, was not beyond question. An anonymous poet poses the query: "How can it profit Christians to learn of the marriage of Philology and Mercury?"[22] The elaborate allegorical setting, it is implied, can be of no use to a Christian.

Similarly, the sciences of the quadrivium were not treated as important in themselves, but arithmetic and astronomy were studied for their usefulness in determining the Church calendar. Music was especially relevant for its function in providing a beautiful setting to the liturgy. Gerbert, with his keen interest in arithmetic and astronomy, and his ingenuity in devising instruments and models for making these subjects understandable to his students, might have turned his talents to experiment in science or mechanics, but he seems never to have considered devoting himself to pure science. Indeed, quite to the contrary, this unrivalled polymath is responsible for the statement that the *ars artium* is the guidance of souls.[23] Notker Labeo, after a long scholarly career during which he made commentaries on a number of the standard works on the arts, said that he was turning away from these pursuits entirely in order to devote himself to theology.[24]

With this basic philosophy directing their lives, the teachers, who had learned the arts largely in Church schools and were in a position to serve the Church, understandably experienced a sense of mission, a feeling of obligation to pass on their learning.[25] Aelfric speaks of the duty of every man who has a valuable skill to make it available to others, "lest God's money be idle and he be called an unprofitable servant, be bound, and cast out into outer darkness."[26] They often quoted the Biblical command, "Freely have ye received, freely give." In another sense they were like missionaries, for they felt that they must be aggressive in combatting error and ignorance. In this role they were sometimes described as "agonistes" or "athletes Dei," God's champion, an epithet applied to Bruno, that staunch "propagator Christianae fidei."[27]

These were dedicated men of faith and good-will, giving their lives to education for the greater glory of God. It is not surprising, then, that many of them were later canonized for the sanctity of their lives and their spiritual gifts. St. Abbo, the martyr, devoted his whole life to teaching and met his death in an abbey in Gascony at the hands of some rebellious monks whose monastery he had gone to reform. While he was still living, St. Wolfgang was venerated as a holy man, and after his death he was honored by numerous shrines. St. Bruno, in his work as archbishop of Cologne, so completely gave himself to the interests, physical and spiritual, of his people that he has won their continued gratitude and reverence.

While the Church thus paid tribute to their holiness, the schoolmasters themselves would seem to have been directing their efforts toward a different goal, that is, of attaining and imparting some vision of the Wisdom of God. Well-versed in the Bible, they often spoke of the Sapiential books, the Psalms and Proverbs, where the supreme virtue of wisdom is defined as "The fear of the Lord is the beginning of wisdom." They were also familiar with the chief patristic interpretations of the Bible and so knew the long tradition whereby the Wisdom of God came to be symbolized by Christ. In their own time, one of their own teachers, Aelfric, in his *Homily on the Birth of Christ,*[28] says, "The Son is the Father's Wisdom, of Him and with Him", also "The Son of Almighty God is eternally begotten of the Father, true light and true wisdom", and finally, there is a prayer to "Our dear Lord Christ, who is the true Wisdom."

This concept of Christ as the symbol of divine Wisdom as it relates to man could in no way be expressed more effectively than it is in a famous drawing reputed to have been made by St. Dunstan himself in a manuscript originally from Glastonbury.[29] Here one sees a towering figure of Christ who holds in his right hand a blossoming rod, the scepter of redemption, that bears its inscription from Psalm XLV.6, in Latin, "The scepter of thy kingdom is a right scepter." In his left hand Christ holds an open book with the text from Psalm XXXIV.11, "Come, ye children, hearken unto me. I will teach you the fear of the Lord." At his feet, a very small figure of Dunstan, prostrate, bears the inscription: "O Christ, I pray, protect me, Dunstan."[30] In his humility, in his expression of complete dependence, and in his vision of the great Wisdom of God, one sees, I believe, a symbolic representation of many of the schoolmasters, particularly in the troubled years as the tenth century began.

Ottonis musica in dyalogo

2. Odo at his writing desk

II

Two Reformer-Teachers

Odo of Cluny
(879-942)

*Chief restorer of the Benedictine Order
and principal reformer of the Rule.*[1]

AMONG THE SCORES of students whom Remigius of Auxerre taught
during his long career of expounding the seven liberal arts when
he had the distinction of being "in divinis et humanis scripturis
eruditissimus,"[2] the one who seems to have exerted the most far-
reaching and long-lasting influence upon education was Odo,[3]
best known as abbot of Cluny. After his first few years of study as
a cleric at the monastery of St. Martin at Tours, when "though a
pupil he began to take the lead in the ranks of the masters,"[4] Odo
went to Paris to study dialectic and music under Remigius.[5]

Later, while still a young man, at the monastery of Baume in
Burgundy, Odo wrote his most important work, the *Collationes*.[6]
In this long treatise, modelled after Augustine's *City of God,* the
two conflicting peoples, the children of Cain and the children of
Abel, are contrasted in their roles in contemporary society. Like a
latter-day Jeremiah, Odo decries the moral disintegration of his
times and inveighs against the vices and depravity that he sees
everywhere, both in the Church and among the powerful of the
laity. In the tradition of Roman satire, he draws a more dismal and
more seemingly hopeless picture of his age, with its nobles who

plunder the poor and its worldly princes of the Church who are heedless of the plight of their people, than the descriptions in many of the later writers. His purpose, like Juvenal's, was to shock his fellow men into action to pull themselves out of the morass into which they had fallen.

Frailer men would have reacted with depression or despair to such darkness and evil which gave unmistakable signs of the approaching destruction of the world. Odo, however, interpreted the signs as a challenge to him to salvage what he could before the end should come. Sustained by his conviction of mission, he devoted the last fifteen years of his life to reforming monasteries that had become demoralized, establishing new ones, and restoring the Benedictine Rule in others throughout France and Italy. His work as a reformer began at the abbey of Cluny where he was called to be abbot in 927. A rare combination of natural administrative ability, boundless energy, and complete fearlessness accounts for his astonishing accomplishments in introducing the reforms he had effected at Cluny into countless other monastic houses, often in the face of great opposition. Among the most conspicuous in France were Fleury-on-the-Loire, Limoges, Clermont, Poitiers, Sens, and Aurillac; in Italy the most notable in Rome were St. Mary's on the Aventine, and outside the walls, St. Paul's, St. Agnes', and St. Laurence's, while beyond Rome were Subiaco, Salerno, and Monte Cassino, the first home of the Benedictine Rule. Of course, Odo's fame rests upon this remarkable achievement, but he deserves recognition also for his great contribution by providing in the monastic establishments suitable schools and by serving as teacher himself.

The only contemporary biography of Odo stresses neither of these lasting monuments to his life work, but rather emphasizes his great spiritual qualities, particularly his remarkable patience maintained under the most trying circumstances, his Christian charity, and his humility, and cites examples of supernatural manifestations during his life and after his death. John, a monk originally from Salerno, who knew Odo during the last four years of his life, his disciple and close companion who accompanied him on his journeys into Italy, wrote the biography[7] as an act of devotion to record "this goodly inheritance for the benefit of posterity."[8] Although Odo had not been canonized, John calls him "our most holy father,"[9] and in the form and substance of the *Vita*, he follows the pattern of the medieval lives of saints.

From John of Salerno's biography and from the brief references in other writers of the next two centuries,[10] one can find evidence to support the thesis that Odo thought of himself primarily as a teacher. In his literary works, in his preaching, and in his music, he seems to have been supplementing the services he performed as *magister*[11] in the classroom. Born into a family of some education and of deep religious convictions, attached to the household of William of Aquitaine, Odo was early entrusted to a priest for his elementary education, but was shortly recalled to be trained as a court page. Because of his special devotion to St. Martin and as a result of an illness which he considered a divine sign, at the age of nineteen Odo entered the monastery of St. Martin at Tours as a cleric. There, though surrounded by indifferent or hostile canons, he eagerly applied himself to learning as well as to religious exercises and soon began to surpass his masters.[12] After an interval spent in Paris studying dialectic and music under Remigius, he returned to Tours. At this time some of the friendly canons urged Odo to make an epitome of the great *Moralia* of St. Gregory, a book widely used and valued for it theological and ethical teachings. When he was reluctant to undertake this task because he feared that the original for which he had great reverence would be neglected for the abridgment, he experienced a vision of St. Gregory in which the saint presented him with a sharpened pen and bade him write the book.[13] Since the clerics who were sufficiently well educated would read the *Moralia* in the original, Odo's epitome was purely a matter of making the subject more compact and more easily understood by the weaker students. Only a dedicated teacher would have performed this long task.[14]

During his years at Tours Odo became increasingly determined to find a monastery where the Rule of St. Benedict was strictly observed. After many journeys through France, with a congenial religious, Adhegrinus, he started for Italy, but in Burgundy, at the monastery of Baume, he thought he had found what he was seeking, for there the Rule of St. Benedict of Nursia was observed along with the revision of St. Benedict of Aniane. Odo presented the library with one hundred books, his sole possession, and received the habit there. His superior knowledge of theology and the arts made it natural that he should be chosen master of the school almost immediately. Only with reluctance he became a priest and shortly after was chosen abbot. Early in his residence at Baume and at the command of his abbot, Odo wrote the didactic treatise which he called *Collationes*.

In 927 he left Baume, where among the older monks he found strong resistance to his efforts to maintain the standards of the Benedictine Rule, to become the second abbot of the newly founded abbey of Cluny. Here he had the task of finishing the church and other buildings as well as the challenge of developing a vigorous community life. Before long he was sought by monasteries all over France and Italy to restore and reform their ruined or demoralized houses. Between his long journeys and the actual work of restoration during which he often encountered extreme hostility and even physical violence, he found time to write a long poem in seven books, which he called *Occupatio,* with the subtitle *Carmen epicodidacticum Christianum.*[15] His theme was the grace of God and the sin of man from the creation of the world to his own times. Here, again, he anticipates the approaching millenium as he inveighs against the evils of society. The immediate purpose, of course, was to instruct his own monks in the seriousness of their situation. Another work composed during his years at Cluny is a *Life of St. Gerald of Aurillac*[16] for Abbot Aymo which he thought of as a memorial to a saintly life but also as a source of inspiration for the instruction of the monks at Aurillac.

Only five sermons of Odo have been printed.[17] These, obviously, were intended for the spiritual edification of the monks at

Cluny, but they are also informative of the lives of the saints whom Odo sought to honor. The sermon on St. Benedict, for example, became such an honored tribute to their patron that the Benedictines continued to read it year after year at the feast of St. Benedict.

Since Odo's special interest and talent lay in music, it is natural that he should employ his knowledge of this art for the instruction of the monks. While he was at Tours, he composed both the words and the music of four hymns in honor of St. Martin and twelve antiphons on the life of the saint for his feast day.[18] In contemporary records, Odo is called *musicus,*[19] and since this term was used to denote a person skilled in the science of numbers in relation to sound, it is not surprising that several treatises on music have traditionally been attributed to him.[20] Although modern critics have shown that some of these may not be his work, two, the *Tonarius* and the *Dialogus de musica,* are still considered authentic.[21] In these technical works Odo the scholar was looking to a wider circle of learners than his own monastery.

For the years that Odo spent as a classroom teacher, unfortunately the records give scanty information. This is not surprising since the Benedictine Order never professed to specialize in education but sought rather to develop a community of dedicated and perfected monks who would also provide the most acceptable Church service to honor God. In the case of Odo, it is known that from the time he entered Tours, he served as instructor to the choir to train the boys for their prominent part in the liturgy. At Baume Odo served as *magister scholae,* presumably teaching not only the elementary skills of reading and writing but supervising all of their religious training, as he indoctrinated them in the Benedictine Rule.

As a schoolmaster Odo had two of the best qualifications: he had as much knowledge as was available at his time, and he understood and loved his pupils. The historian Rodulfus Glaber, in the eleventh century, calls Odo *sapientissimus* as well as *religiosissimus,*[22] and Adémar, a century later, names him *litteris adprime liberalibus eruditus.*[23] Since only Abbo and Gerbert in the tenth century are known to have mastered all seven of the liberal arts, these testimonials to Odo's learning are very significant. John of Salerno, who was greatly impressed by Odo's extensive knowledge, reports that when he first went to Tours, the lazy canons like old crows unceasingly cawed their disapproval of his constant study.[24] He also says that Odo was sought out by visitors from afar and that he "offered to all the cup they so much desired, and as from an open book gave fitting instruction to all."[25] Even at Baume, the best religious house he could find, many of the monks persecuted him, trying to drive him away because of his superior knowledge which, ironically, he had so freely offered them.

That Odo understood children is apparent in John's story about the journeys he took in Odo's company. He says that whenever they met any boys along the way, Odo asked them to sing for him, then rewarded them as if to pay for their performance.[26] Odo's remarkable gift of laughter and his ability to awaken it in others must have been an asset to his teaching, especially when some were reluctant to learn.[27] Even though he could relax the tensions of nervous boys with his light touch, Odo was convinced of the efficacy of the rod as a stimulus at the proper times.[28] It is interesting to note that he speaks of God's use of the schoolmaster's rod to correct sinners and bring them back to the right path.[29] Odo's biographer apparently did not consider it relevant to his purpose to cite instances of Odo's instruction of older scholars, so he mentions only in an incidental way the fact that once at St. Paul's in Rome the abbot asked him to correct the text of a dialogue on the life of St. Martin and to write a commentary on it. Odo immediately agreed to do this, but there the account ends.[30]

Unsatisfactory as is the available information concerning Odo's classroom teaching, he must still be counted among the first of the teachers of the tenth century. In the numerous religious houses that he restored and reformed,[31] he provided a milieu favorable to study and he instituted schools for training a long succession of monks. Aside from John of Salerno, however, names of his pupils

are not recorded, but from the monasteries he restored, in a later generation, there came two of the greatest schoolmasters of the century, Abbo of Fleury and Gerbert of Aurillac.

Everaclus of Liège
(ca. 887-971)

Wisdom like that of Solomon shone forth on the face of this learned man.[32]

The wave of enthusiasm activated by the reforms of Odo and the Cluniac monks in France and Italy soon touched the lands to the north and east where the revival of religious zeal expressed itself in somewhat different ways.[33] In Lower Lotharingia an idealistic young man, Gerard,[34] rebuilt an old church in his native village near the Meuse and founded a house for canons which shortly became a Benedictine monastery at Brogne. His success in establishing a place where devoted monks could develop their spiritual lives encouraged Gilbert, duke of Lotharingia, to enlist his aid in restoring another religious house, the old abbey of St. Ghislain, that had fallen into decay. In Ghent two more once-famous abbeys, St. Peter's and St. Bavon's, were reformed by Gerard with the help of Arnulf, count of Flanders, and in France also Gerard restored two monasteries. In all, he is credited with the reclamation of eighteen monastic houses between the years 914 and 953.

About the same time, in Upper Lotharingia, in the diocese of Metz, the reform movement was centered in the monastery of Gorze under the guidance of a dedicated monk, John of Vandières, better known as John of Gorze.[35] With the aid of a sympathetic bishop, Adalbero of Metz, John restored the old ruined monastery into a model community and made it a "beehive" of spiritual life which attracted religious from all over Europe. Before his death in 974, he had reformed over seventy religious houses, chiefly in Trier, Toul, Metz, and in the diocese of Liège.

Neither of these two reformers exhibited the interest in teaching that Odo had felt was so important. Although John had been taught in his youth at Metz by Blidulfus, a pupil of Remigius, and at St. Mihiel by Hildeboldus, another pupil of Remigius, he said that he had profited very little by this training. His later self-education was confined almost entirely to reading the Bible and the Fathers. The biographers fail to mention any monastic schools, but these must have been instituted to train the boys to read and to sing in order to participate in the services of the Church, and some theological studies must have been provided for the older monks. Anything comparable to the education given in the monasteries during the ninth century was certainly missing, however, for one finds that this important aspect of monastic life in the diocese of Liège, at any rate, became the concern of the bishops. One of the bishops who was chiefly responsible for restoring the schools in the monasteries was Everaclus,[36] who served the diocese of Liège from 959 to 971.[37]

The most convincing testimony to the effectiveness of Everaclus' work as a teacher is found in a letter[38] written by an Anglo-Saxon monk, who identifies himself only as "B," to Ethelgar, archbishop of Canterbury, about 988, seventeen years after Everaclus' death. "B" says that he had studied under Everaclus in Liège where the beloved master introduced him and many others to a banquet of sacred studies. Expressing his grief and despair at Everaclus' death, he says that now he is ever hungry and always thirsty for the divine wisdom of which he had had but a taste. To explain this unsatisfied craving, he quotes Ecclesiasticus (XXIV, 29) where Wisdom says, "Those who eat me will still hunger, and those who drink me will still thirst." Obviously a teacher who could inspire such an insatiable desire for learning was a very gifted master.

It is interesting to note that the writers of the chronicles of Liege[39] who record Everaclus' episcopal activities, as well as his biographer, Reinerus,[40] who used the chronicles as his source, devote a very large proportion of their accounts to the work of

Everaclus in establishing schools and to incidents relating to his teaching. They record that he was born into a noble family of Saxon origin and went first to school at Cologne. For more advanced study in the secular arts and in theology he went to Liège where he studied under one of the most brilliant of scholars, the ill-fated Ratherius of Verona.[41] There he gained the reputation of being without equal in scholarship.[42] He early showed his unusual talent for teaching at Bonn, "that Verona of the north," where he attracted a great flood of students. According to his biographer, he showed the greatest consideration for the boys' inexperience and timidity; he not only expected to be questioned by them, but he insisted upon it, never growing bored or tired. He stimulated the dull and slothful by quoting appropriate passages from Proverbs and in a joking manner by reciting satirical lines from the *Epistles* of Horace.[43]

In 959, at the wish of the Emperor Otto I, Everaclus was consecrated bishop of Liège by Bruno, archbishop of Cologne, who rejoiced that "such a flame was being placed upon the candelabrum of the Church of Liège."[44] When he found that his new duties would include restoring the cathedral school[45] which had earlier enjoyed great prestige, he wrote a most cordial letter to his old teacher, Ratherius, asking him to come and assume the duties of master, even adding that he himself would not be embarrassed to become his pupil and submit to his discipline.[46] Although Ratherius did not accept the invitation, under Everaclus' supervision the cathedral school, to which he added a new school dedicated to St. Martin, soon became of first importance in all of northeastern Europe. Throughout the diocese of Liège Everaclus restored or instituted schools, developed suitable courses of study, called qualified teachers to train the pupils, and even provided adequate remuneration for them from his own resources.

Everaclus' zeal for these schools was so great that he never allowed any other duties to keep him from visiting them often and attending the classes. Frequently he taught the older boys himself, using every means he could devise to stimulate them to want to learn. Recognizing the disparate abilities and experience of the boys, he tried to make the lessons suit their individual needs. With the slow to learn he was patient and gentle, willing to explain a thing over and over again until the matter was clear.[47] Often, of course, he was called away on official business, but he never forgot his schools. At such times he used to correspond with the masters, sending them his own literary compositions, sometimes in poetry and again in prose, in an effort to keep vital their interest in study. His constant efforts bore fruit, for many of the boys, even the most unpromising, in a short time acquired some knowledge of secular learning and Church doctrine.[48]

In the midst of heavy responsibilities, Everaclus took every opportunity to increase his own knowledge, which included not only the arts of the trivium and theology, but also at least some of the sciences of the quadrivium. His biographer describes an incident in which Everaclus' knowledge of astronomy proved very useful. When he was with the emperor in Calabria in 968, a solar eclipse occurred and there was general panic as even the bravest men in the army of Otto I rushed for any shelter available, thinking that the end of the world was at hand. When the light began to reappear and they emerged from their hiding places, Everaclus was able to reassure them as he explained the phenomenon.[49]

After Everaclus' death, his body was entombed before the high altar in the Church of St. Martin which he had established. His biographer[50] gives as a kind of requiem most suitable for him as schoolmaster, the words spoken to Daniel: "And they that be wise shall shine as the brightness of the firmament, and they that turn many to righteousness as the stars for ever and ever."[51]

III

Three English Monastic Bishops

LEGEND DRAMATIZES the restoration of monasticism and the revival of schools in England by associating the movement with two incidents in which kings were the principal actors. It is said that about 940 King Edmund, after a miraculous escape from death while hunting on the cliffs of Cheddar, as an act of thanksgiving made Dunstan abbot of the church at Glastonbury with the injunction that he foster Christian worship and carry out the Rule of St. Benedict.[1] Another tradition makes King Edgar the hero as he fulfilled a vow made in early childhood when, shocked upon seeing the ruins of a magnificent monastery, he promised that he would one day restore the great religious houses of England to their former glory.[2] The first step toward this goal was made when he elevated Dunstan to the status of bishop in 957.[3]

No one would underrate the prime importance of the sympathy and support of the kings, but greater credit for the resurgence of monasticism and the rehabilitation of the cloister schools must be assigned to a constellation of prominent monks who became bishops: Dunstan, Ethelwold, and Oswald. These "three brilliant lights" of the Church, as an eleventh-century chronicle calls them, "shining from their great candelabra at Canterbury, Winchester, and Worcester, so illuminated the three corners of England that they seemed to eclipse the very stars."[4] Fortunately contemporary biographies of St. Dunstan, archbishop of Canterbury,[5] St. Ethelwold, bishop of Winchester,[6] and St. Oswald, bishop of Worcester and archbishop of York,[7] all written by men who knew them, give accounts of their activities in restoring monasteries, in reforming monastic practices, and in promoting learning.

3. King Edgar, St. Dunstan, and St. Ethelwold with the Regularis Concordia

St. Dunstan
(ca. 909-988)

History shows that a combination of fortunate circumstances—
his high birth, his love for learning, and his zeal for the monastic
life—made Dunstan the natural leader in renewing monasticism
in England.[8] Dunstan was born in Somerset of noble and wealthy
Christian parents related to the royal family. As a young boy he
was taken to nearby Glastonbury to be taught at the holy and very
famous abbey whose buildings at that time had badly deteriorated
and whose remaining clerics had so far departed from discipline
that monasticism was virtually extinct. Somehow, Dunstan, in his
eagerness to learn, found men to instruct him in the elementary
secular and sacred subjects, but independently he read whatever
books he could find in the neglected library of the abbey. This
introduction to theology confirmed his determination to become a
monk, and he soon received the tonsure. A large part of his
education seems to have come from the Irish monks who visited
Glastonbury on pilgrimage to the shrine of St. Patrick. With these
learned scholars who were well trained in the liberal arts and
philosophy, Dunstan studied Holy Scripture and the secular arts as
well. They taught him to read the works of the poets and orators,
and they gave him practice in writing Latin and speaking it
effectively. No doubt he also learned a little Greek. It was
certainly from them that Dunstan learned something of the
sciences of arithmetic, geometry, astronomy, and music.[9] In
applied music he acquired great skill in playing the harp, the
organ, and the wind instruments.[10] From the books of these Irish
pilgrims he was able to study more deeply the works of the Fathers
and the lives of the saints, but especially to relate all of his
knowledge to the Bible. This close application to study most
unfortunately made him the object of persecution at the hands of
the clerics who must have felt his zeal and his industry a reproach
to their indifference.

Dunstan's stay at Glastonbury was interrupted by a period of residence at the court of King Athelstan where he was introduced to the worldly pursuits appropriate for a courtier and future diplomat. Yet he still found time for reading theology though he was busy acquiring new skills, such as the art of calligraphy and illuminating manuscripts, and carving, as well as the crafts of the potter and the metalsmith.[11] After eight or nine years his studies again made trouble for him as he was accused of inquiring into the occult sciences, and was dismissed from court. The next five years spent in the quiet of Glastonbury where as a solitary he observed a monastic regimen, or at Winchester with the wise old Bishop Aelfheah, his kinsman, who ordained him priest, were probably the most important ones in Dunstan's life, for during that time he came to the realization that the Benedictine Rule must be restored in England and that he must be the one to initiate such a movement. Thus, when about 940, King Edmund made him abbot of Glastonbury,[12] he saw clearly what his mission must be. His program started with the restoration of the old buildings and the addition of others necessary for community life, new chapels and a church. One of his greatest concerns was with the training of the boys and men who came to make their religious profession. Under Dunstan's supervision in the school not only monastic discipline and sacred studies but the arts of the trivium and of the quadrivium and even manual skills were taught. Although details concerning the subjects are lacking, William of Malmesbury in his biography of Dunstan gives some information. He says that when the gifted and noble young Ethelwold was seeking a monastery where he could find both study and the enforcement of the Rule, although many other monasteries wished to receive him, he chose Glastonbury so that he might have the guidance of his friend Dunstan.[13] There he studied grammar and poetry and made his profession. Another clue to the teaching at Glastonbury comes from three manuscripts, now in the Bodleian Library, that once belonged to Dunstan.[14] The first is the famous "classbook" of Dunstan with a portrait of the bishop prostrate before Christ as divine Wisdom;[15] it contains a work of Latin grammar, miscellaneous texts on number, tables and texts on the computation of the date of Easter, liturgical lessons and canticles, and passages from the Prophets in Greek with the Latin translation. The second contains a commentary on the Apocalypse, and a third has a collection of legal and canonical texts.

One must assume that Dunstan, who had the reputation for great learning,[16] assembled all of the books then available to him for the instruction of the throng of applicants who sought his house during the fifteen years he labored there. William of Malmesbury records that the library of Glastonbury had an abundance of beautiful old books.[17] In a list of books belonging to the library in 1247, those labelled "Vetustissimi" may have been there in Dunstan's time. They include Bibles, the Church Fathers, theological works, sermons, lives of saints, and Latin grammars.[18] Dunstan's biographer is less concerned with listing books than with noting the results of his work in preparing his students to go forth and restore other monasteries. He says that as abbot he trained countless young men who became priors, deans, abbots, bishops, and even archbishops.

Political difficulties that caused Dunstan to leave his country and to go to Flanders to Count Arnulf in the year 956 proved to have a great influence for good in the revival of monasticism in England. In Ghent he had an opportunity to live in the monastery of St. Peter's that had earlier been restored by Gerard of Brogne, where the strict Benedictine Rule was observed. This experience, along with his association with men who were responsible for the revival and propagation of monasticism, gave Dunstan new courage for his work in England. When, a year later, King Edgar recalled him and made him bishop, first of Worcester and then of London, and two years later elevated him to archbishopric of Canterbury, Dunstan was ready to put into effect his plans for making the monasteries "the very spiritual and intellectual heart of the nation."[19] History has not preserved a list of the houses directly renewed or founded by Dunstan and his disciples, but they include Malmesbury, St. Augustine's, Canterbury, St. Peter's, Westminster, St. Peter's, Bath, Muchelney, and Athelney.

After 960 when Dunstan, upon his enthronement as archbishop of Canterbury, went to Rome and received the pallium at the hands of Pope John XII, his duties as Primate of England were sufficient to engage his days completely, yet he was constantly visiting the monasteries, supervising the building and overseeing the training of the monks. Furthermore, as chief counselor to the king, Dunstan had to spend a great deal of time at court, where he had a large part in framing the secular as well as the ecclesiastical legislation that was enacted. After King Edgar's death in 975, Dunstan crowned King Edward, the Younger, who lived only a few years, and he also officiated at the coronation of Ethelred II.

Amid all these distracting secular demands, he still tried to live the monastic life, but only in his last years he once more had time to continue with the occupations he had found so satisfying. His daily routine was that of a monk as he observed all of the offices. He renewed his skill in making musical instruments, particularly organs and bells. He may also have composed music at this time as he had done earlier in his life, when he always considered this gift the result of some heavenly vision rather than of his own talent.[20] Early in the morning he worked at correcting faulty manuscripts that had been written at the monastery. He listened to all who came to him for advice, help, or instruction. He served as arbiter for all kinds of legal suits and settled many misunderstandings. Young and old, men and women, clergy and lay people came to hear his teaching. "And so all this land of England was filled with his holy teaching, shining before God and men like the sun and the moon."[21]

St. Ethelwold
(ca. 908 - 984)

It is said that Dunstan once had a vision in which he saw in the midst of the cloister at Glastonbury a great tree which gave shade to the whole of England. Its branches were laden with monks' habits and at the top a habit with a very wide cowl overshadowed all the others. Interpreting the dream, an old priest said that the tree represented the island of Glastonbury, while the habits were the monks, and the great cowl was Ethelwold who was destined to become the greatest in all of England. As the years passed and the prophecy was being fulfilled, the chronicler says that the achievements of Ethelwold redounded to the honor of his teacher, Dunstan, for "the glory of the father is a wise son."[22] But the relationship of Dunstan and Ethelwold was more properly that of friend to friend, for they were almost exact contemporaries and shared many significant experiences in their careers.

Ethelwold's life was recorded by his most scholarly disciple, Aelfric, abbot of Eynsham, probably about the year 1004.[23] Some time afterwards, an enlarged version almost entirely dependent upon Aelfric, was prepared anonymously, probably by Wulfstan, the precentor of Winchester.[24] Ethelwold was born in Winchester about 908, the son of noble parents from whom he inherited a devotion to the Christian religion. From boyhood he interested himself in studying and early won the attention of King Athelstan who invited him to his court. Here he met Dunstan and with him studied under Bishop Aelfheah of Winchester, by whom both young men were ordained on the same day. Here he apparently learned some of the practical skills of working with metals and constructing musical instruments which he later used for the great benefit of his churches.

Shortly after Dunstan became abbot of Glastonbury, Ethelwold, at the command of the king, went to him to be taught the Benedictine way of life and to be received by him as a monk. The monastic life suited him well and he brought to it all of his energy

4. St. Ethelwold blessing the Cathedral of Winchester

and zeal. In addition to theology and sacred studies, he learned from Dunstan many secular subjects, though the biographer mentions only grammar, the art of metrics, sacred books, and classical authors. It had been Ethelwold's wish to go to the Continent to the monastery of St. Benedict at Fleury, that model house which had been reformed by Odo of Cluny, in order to experience what he considered the perfect monastic life. King Edred, however, was not willing to lose such a brilliant mind from England, so he offered him the position of abbot of the old but ruined abbey of Abingdon in Berkshire.

The nine years (954-963) that Ethelwold labored at Abingdon constituted perhaps the most fruitful period in the history of the reformation of the monasteries and hence of the restoration of learning in England. With serveral monks from Glastonbury and two from other monasteries, and with the help of the king, Ethelwold immediately undertook the building of a church, the rebuilding of the decayed cloister, and the establishment of the Benedictine Rule. In order to improve the monastic life at Abingdon he sent his best educated monk, Osgar, to Fleury to observe the practices followed there. At the same time, to perfect the musical parts of the Church services, he sent to the French abbey of Corbie, renowned for its music, asking for monks to come to train the choir. When these changes were effected and Abingdon had become a successful monastery, young men from all over England came to experience its rigorous religious and intellectual training. It may have been during this period that Ethelwold had charge of the education of the young King Edgar, for the historian says that "he instructed the king in the knowledge of the true King."[25] Tradition says that Ethelwold was determined to make the Church of St. Mary as beautiful as possible, so from his own resources, he gave a large golden chalice and three crosses of gold and silver. With his own skilful hands he made an organ, bells, crosses, and a wheel of gold that supported twelve lamps and little bells. For the back of the altar he made a retable of gold and silver with figures of the twelve Apostles carved upon it.[26]

When Dunstan, archbishop of Canterbury at this time, saw what remarkable changes Ethelwold had accomplished at Abingdon, he urged King Edgar to appoint him bishop of Winchester, and he had the satisfaction of consecrating his old friend. Since the days when both had studied at Winchester, several weak bishops had allowed the discipline to be neglected, and the three religious houses were in the hands of demoralized clerics. Immediately Ethelwold began the difficult work of clearing away the abuses, banishing the more recalcitrant priests, and renewing true monastic life in the Old Minster, the New Minster, and the Nuns' Minster. When finally novices who wished the Benedictine way of life were installed, Ethelwold could at last give his attention to teaching and studying. He found time to teach the boys and young men and even translated books into English for them; by his friendly conversations with them, he inspired them always to higher achievements. The success of his methods can be judged by the number of his disciples who became abbots and bishops throughout England. About this time, at the request of King Edgar, he translated the Rule of St. Benedict into English for the benefit of those monks who had no Latin.[27]

With the monks well provided for and the schools in order, Ethelwold, always a builder, could give more of his time to supervising the rebuilding of the great cathedral. Although it was not completed in his lifetime, he had the satisfaction of presiding over the solemn ceremony of the entombment of the relics of St. Swithin in a fitting shrine in the cathedral in 971. Also during these last years Ethelwold restored or reformed at least eight monasteries, of which the most famous are those of Ely, Peterborough, and Thorney. Fortunately the records of the monastery of Ely give a rather full account of the bishop's extraordinary efforts in rebuilding and restoring that old monastery in the fen country, founded by St. Etheldreda three centuries earlier.[28] Ethelwold bought not only the land but also neighboring estates to add to it, then enriched it with splendid gifts. With Dunstan in 970 he consecrated as abbot Brihtnoth whom he had trained at

Abingdon. Peterborough, an even older religious house than Ely, had been in ruins for a century before Ethelwold bought the site and rebuilt a fine monastery. His generosity provided the church with rich vestments, gold and silver crossess, bells, candlesticks and other necessary altar furnishings, including an Evangeliary. A list of twenty books in Latin that Ethelwold donated to the monastery is of more than usual interest because it gives some indication of the studies that were pursued there.[29] Three of the books were on theology, one of which was *On the Eucharist;* four were lives of early saints; four were works of Biblical exegesis, including Bede's *Commentary on Mark* and Remigius of Auxerre's *Interpretations of the Hebrew Names;* three were purely secular, the most important of which was a *Commentary on Martianus Capella,* an indispensable aid for teaching the seven liberal arts; four might be classed as popular—a book on medicine, one on miracles, one on prognostications, and a bestiary; in a class by itself is a long poem by Abbo of St. Germain, *On the Siege of Paris,* written in 896 and probably brought from the Continent by some of the monks who visited Abingdon. Finally there was a book on Greek letters, a fact that tends to support the belief that Ethelwold had some knowledge of Greek, which he may have acquired from Dunstan, who, in turn, may have learned it from the Irish pilgrim monks at Glastonbury.[30]

In addition to Ely and Peterborough, Ethelwold rebuilt a third monastery in Cambridgeshire in the remote fens on the island of Thorney. A small church, a small cloister for a very few monks who sought a solitary life, it became a favorite of Ethelwold. He gave it spiritual enrichment by transferring there the remains of earlier holy men who had been associated with the place. When the Rule was well established, he settled one of his most talented Winchester monks, Godeman, there as abbot.

While he was still at Winchester, Godeman had called Ethelwold *Boanerges,* son of thunder, an epithet that Christ had applied to his energetic disciples, James and his brother John. The name seems to have been particularly appropriate for the tireless bishop as he kept watch over all of the monasteries with their schools that he had worked to establish. His biographer says that he regularly visited each of the monasteries to ensure their rigid adherence to the Rule, taking counsel with those monks who were obedient but correcting the erring with lashings. He was as frightening as a lion to the disobedient and undisciplined, but more gentle than a dove to the obedient and humble.

Very convincing testimony to the effectiveness of Ethelwold's teaching and energetic sponsorship of the monastery schools is a magnificent manuscript written and illuminated by Godeman while a monk at Winchester, at his request about 980. Now in the British Library,[31] this great Benedictional or book of solemn episcopal blessings for the liturgical year consists of one hundred nineteen folios with twenty-eight full-page miniatures. The beautiful Caroline minuscule script (which may have been introduced into England through Dunstan's influence to replace the old Anglo-Saxon script) is firm and clear and altogether professional in its uniformity. The sureness of the drawings and the delicacy and appropriateness of the colors reveal Godeman as a mature and experienced artist. The manner of portrayal of the saints would seem to indicate that these miniatures were painted by an artist who was also a scholar, for many of them are shown holding books. For example, in a group of three confessors, two have books; all six of the Virgin Saints are represented with books; ten of the Apostles hold books; St. Etheldreda, foundress and abbess of Ely, has a blossoming branch but also a book; St. Swithin, early bishop of Winchester, and St. Benedict have their books. For Trinity Sunday Christ in Majesty is represented as Wisdom enthroned, giving a blessing with his right hand and holding a book in his left. Most surprising is the Epiphany scene where the Infant Christ is portrayed blessing the magi with his right hand and holding a book in his left. The last miniature represents a bishop, probably Ethelwold himself, pronouncing a blessing at the dedication of a church which may be the rebuilt cathedral of Winchester. He is reading from a golden book, the

Benedictional, held by one of three monks, each of whom is holding a book.[32]

St. Oswald
(ca. 930 - 992)

The biographer of the third of the English monastic bishops, Oswald, declares that as Homer and Virgil sang of great men so he will celebrate the noble, heroic, and saintly bishop.[33] The anonymous *Life,* written about the end of the tenth century, was the work of a monk who knew and loved Oswald and was familiar with his favorite monastery, Ramsey.[34] This full account of his life, supplemented by a detailed history of the abbey of Ramsey in the *Historia Rameseiensis,*[35] furnishes a very complete picture of his activities in reforming and restoring monasticism in northern England.

Born of a distinguished family of Danish origin, nephew to two archbishops, Oswald as a boy showed an unusual thirst for knowledge, marked ability in learning, and a strong inclination toward the religious life. In Canterbury under the care of his uncle, Archbishop Odo, he had the most learned teacher available, Frithegode,[36] who excelled in both religious and secular studies. From him Oswald must have learned theology, some of the liberal arts, and possibly Greek.[37] To encourage his nephew's vocation, Odo early settled Oswald as a canon in a small monastery in Winchester, but as the unregulated life and worldly pursuits that flourished there made the place unsatisfactory to him, he sought permission to go to France to the monastery of Fleury to learn the true Benedictine way of life.

The five or six years Oswald spent at Fleury served to train him for the duties he was to assume back in England. He entered upon the strict monastic life with enthusiasm and sincerity. He memorized all of the offices; his beautiful voice and his love for singing made him a valued participant in all of the services. Along with other English monks, notably Germanus from Winchester and Osgar who had been sent there from Abingdon by Ethelwold, he studied both secular and theological subjects and was received into the Benedictine Order before he had to go back to England at the death of his uncle.

Shortly after his return in 958, another uncle, Osketel, archbishop of York, presented him to Dunstan who immediately recognized in the young monk a most valuable assistant in his program of restoring the Benedictine Rule. With the consent of King Edgar, Dunstan elevated Oswald to the bishopric of Worcester which he himself had just left. Not only did Oswald's magnificent voice and eloquence attract so many listeners that he was obliged to build a new cathedral, but as more and more young men came to learn from him the Benedictine way, he sent to Fleury to ask his friend Germanus to come to help with the work, particularly teaching. Before long he transferred Germanus with twelve monks to a small abbey near Bristol, Westbury-on-Trym, where the full Benedictine Rule was strictly observed. This small house could neither receive all of the young men who came seeking the religous life, nor did it satisfy Oswald's aspirations to serve the Church more fully, so he set out to find a perfect situation for a model monastery. Finally, in 968, in Huntingdonshire with the gift of land in Ramsey from an influential nobleman, he made plans for his abbey, and with the help of Dunstan, Ethelwold, and the king, he built a larger church and a monastery, an undertaking which took many years, but finally he dedicated the church in 974. At Ramsey, under the guidance of Germanus as prior, the abbey soon gained the reputation of giving the best training in the Benedictine discipline of all the English monasteries.

Although the biographer is silent about the library at Ramsey, certainly Oswald must have collected books that were needed in the school. What some of these books were it is possible to judge from the copious writings of Byrhtferth, a monk who spent his whole life at the abbey. This scholar, whose special interest was mathematics, shows his acquaintance with the Roman poets, Terence, Horace, Virgil, Lucan, Persius, and Juvenal; with the Church Fathers, Ambrose, Augustine, Clement, and Eusebius; with the encyclopedists, Varro, Martianus Capella, Macrobius, and Isidore of Seville; and particularly with all the scientific works of Bede.[38] It would have been very unusual if Oswald had not also established a scriptorium for the copying of books. Apparently there was a scriptorium where not only copying but fine art work was executed on choice manuscripts. By a singular good fortune one very beautiful book that was produced at Ramsey is now preserved in the British Library.[39] Written sometime between 974 and 986, it is known as the Psalter of Oswald.[40] The script is clear and harmonious and the volume is particularly distinguished by a masterly drawing of the Crucifixion.

In the years following, Oswald became increasingly occupied with administrative duties. He was consecrated archbishop of York in 972, a position he held while still continuing as bishop of Worcester. During this time, no matter how exhausting his other responsibilities were, and sometimes with the help of Ethelwold, he succeeded in restoring or reforming seven more monasteries, including Winchcombe in Gloucestershire and Pershore and Evesham in Worcestershire.

Apart from administering the Rule in the various monasteries that he visited regularly, apparently Oswald did not teach. Instead he gave his attention to finding the best possible teachers with the best possible education. So, for his favorite monastery, Ramsey, he sent a delegation to Fleury begging that a learned monk capable of instructing his novices be sent to England. Abbo, the most learned of all, accepted the invitation and spent two years teaching the liberal arts and theology, chiefly at Ramsey, [41] but also more briefly at other houses. As a teacher, Abbo was most successful in gaining the affection of his students and in inspiring them with a desire to learn. For example, at the request of the monks at Ramsey, he wrote a treatise on Latin grammatical questions. He also added to their knowledge of their own history by writing a life of St. Edmund from the account he had once heard Dunstan relate. He met Ethelwold and enjoyed his warm friendship and was ordained a priest by Oswald. Monks and bishops alike wished to keep Abbo in England. When he was recalled by his abbot in 987, Dunstan, Oswald and the monks from Ramsey and the other houses where he had taught presented him with rich gifts of gold and silver for his monastery. Even after his departure, the monks of Canterbury sent a request that he write a life of Dunstan in poetry. One of the most tangible results of the two brief years he spent in England was the scholarly activity of the monk Byrhtferth whom he had taught at Ramsey.

Throughout his life Oswald continued to be a kind of "beloved disciple" of Dunstan. So, thirteen years after he had assumed power, Dunstan as archbishop of Canterbury, assisted by Oswald, the archbishop of York, officiated at the solemn coronation of King Edgar at Bath in 973.[42] For the dedication of new abbeys, the consecration of bishops, and for countless other ceremonies, Dunstan seems to have called upon Oswald. More significant in revealing the true harmony of mind that existed between the two is the fact that both fulfilled their monastic vows as completely as possible during the years when their episcopal duties kept them from their monasteries, and when old age permitted them to return to the abbeys they had founded, they resumed the life according to the Rule.

By a happy coincidence, the most vigorous years of the lives of the three monastic bishops, Dunstan, Ethelwold, and Oswald, fell in the reign of King Edgar, known as the "Peaceful," who gave his full support to the new movement of restoration and reform which he must have felt promised the spiritual and intellectual salvation of England. Besides his enthusiastic encouragement and his financial assistance in supporting the colony houses at the three chief centers of Glastonbury, Abingdon, and Ramsey, his influence in providing the means for securing uniformity of practice in all the English religious houses was of the greatest importance.

The original Rule of St. Benedict had been known in all the monasteries, and the reinterpretation of the Rule by Benedict of Aniane, used on the Continent since 817, had been introduced into England through the various contacts with Flanders and Burgundy, but the observances differed widely from one monastery to another. Hence, at Winchester at Whitsuntide in the year 970,[43] King Edgar held an unusual Council, perhaps at the instigation of Oswald, but planned and carried out by Dunstan, which was attended by English bishops, abbots and abbesses, and monks from Ghent and Fleury. Here a great code called the *Regularis Concordia,*[44] or the *Monastic Agreement of the Monks and Nuns of the English Nation,* drafted by Ethelwold,[45] was drawn up for the uniform regulation of all English religious houses, and with the adoption of this *Concordia* a new era in the spiritual and cultural life of England began.[46] From medieval to modern times, scholars have regarded as of the utmost importance the work which the king and his bishops undertook and heroically accomplished. Aelfric, for example, looking back to the time of King Edgar, wrote,

> And we say of a truth that the time was blessed and winsome in England, when King Edgar furthered Christianity, and built many monasteries, and his kingdom still continued at peace.[47]

Summing up the intellectual achievements of the three bishops, Dom David Knowles says, "In the sphere of letters, the example of teaching given by Dunstan and Ethelwold made their foundations the home of all the learning possessed by England between the days of Athelstan and those of the Confessor. In the half century that elapsed after the synod at Winchester a blossoming took place at Winchester and Ramsey which must have exceeded the most sanguine expectations of the founders."[48]

IV

St. Abbo of Fleury
(ca. 940-1004)

*There was nothing in life more pleasant
than to learn and to teach.*[1]

TWO LASTING MEMORIALS of the unusually cordial relationship
between the Benedictine monks of the English abbey of Ramsey
and those of the French monastery of Fleury that resulted from the
short visit of Abbo to England are some Latin verses written by
Abbo and a fine manuscript presented to him when he returned to
France. The little elegiac poem (with Virgilian echoes) appended
to the *Grammatical Questions* (534) which he prepared for his "most
beloved English brethren in Christ" is an appreciative description
of the natural beauty of Ramsey with its marshes and ponds
abounding in fish and eels, its shady woodlands, and the vast
expanse of the heavens, affording a clear view of the northern
constellations. The manuscript, a magnificent volume known as
the *Sacramentary of Winchcombe*,[2] is now in the municipal library of
Orléans. It is thought to have been written by Oswald's friend,
Germanus, who was first prior at Ramsey and then abbot of
Winchcombe.[3] A colophon written later at Fleury bears the
message that it was brought from overseas and threatens a most
dire malediction upon anyone who removes it from the
monastery.

The abbey of St. Benedict at Fleury in the valley of the Loire,
which had first gained fame during the reign of Charlemagne
under the poet-abbot, Theodulfus, had suffered vicissitudes

41

similar to those experienced by the English monasteries in the ninth and early tenth centuries. It had accepted the reform of Odo only with extreme reluctance, yet it achieved great distinction as a religious and cultural center by the last half of the tenth century. Fleury was recognized by Pope Gregory V as the first abbey of all Gaul,[4] primarily because the monastery held the relics of St. Benedict, but also because of the fame of its school. The reputation of the school was established largely by Abbo who was, according to his pupil, Odolricus, abbot of St. Martial of Limoges, "the most illustrious master in all France in both sacred and secular studies."[5] In this teacher, in the estimation of one historian (probably Adémar de Chabannes), Wisdom had so well chosen her home that he was considered a supreme authority on all questions throughout France, Germany, and England, indeed a veritable Solomon. Though born and bred in France, he was a true Roman in eloquence, a kind of second Cicero. So great was his wisdom that, besides being supported by the columns of the seven arts, he was an adornment to the whole Church. Every word he uttered seemed not human, but almost divine (377-378).

Information concerning the life and achievements of Abbo is derived chiefly from a biography written by one of his most talented and devoted disciples, Aimoin of Fleury (387-414). Born of free parents in Orléans, Abbo was taken when quite young, "almost from the very cradle" (424), to the abbey of Fleury and several years later became an oblate there under abbot Wulfadus. The seriousness of his religious vocation, the keenness of his intelligence, and his quickness to learn became manifest early. He had only to hear a thing explained once and he had it in his mind forever. His relations with the other boys were friendly, and he showed excellent judgment in choosing his companions, but he enjoyed more his association with the masters. His religious duties did not suffer from his intense application to the study of the liberal arts, for his spiritual life was always foremost.

When Abbo had mastered all of the learning that the teachers could provide him, though he was probably not more than sixteen years old, he was given the responsibility of teaching the younger pupils in reading and chanting. This would include teaching them to read and write, and to read aloud with correct pronunciation; teaching them to chant would mean preparing the boys to participate in the complicated liturgical services. He undertook this assignment in the joyful spirit of one who has found a way to repay his debt, but after several years he became increasingly aware of the insufficiency of his own education. In addition to his training in grammar, arithmetic, and dialectic, he wished to complete his knowledge of the seven liberal arts. He went, then, to the cathedral schools in Paris and in Rheims, both of which had enjoyed the highest reputation under Remigius of Auxerre, but his expectations were not fulfilled for he could find instruction only in astronomy in Rheims. Thereafter he spent some time at Orléans where he took private lessons in music, though at a high price, and even then he felt obliged to hide his knowledge from the envious.

Disappointed at having failed to master all seven arts, Abbo returned to Fleury, "hungering," his biographer says, for fuller knowledge of rhetoric and geometry. From manuscripts he had found in Paris and those in the unusually good library at Fleury, he studied the works of earlier writers in those two fields. He was placed in charge of the monastery school by Abbot Richard about 965. Presumably he taught all seven arts, a rare accomplishment and one which gained him wide acclaim,[6] but there remain written records of his teaching in only three areas: dialectic, astronomy, and arithmetic.

Abbo's teaching career in France was interrupted for two years (985-987) when he was sent to England as a visiting scholar at the invitation of Oswald, archbishop of York.[7] There he taught the Rule and the liberal arts to the monks at Ramsey, but he made shorter visits to other monasteries and was entertained at the king's court and at bishops' palaces. It is said that he kindled in many nobles the desire for the religious life.[8] Although he was successful in his teaching and was greatly admired and loved by the English, he felt exiled and homesick. Before his recall to

France, he had written a treatise on Latin grammar for the Ramsey monks, an edifying life of the martyr king, St. Edmund, and three poems to Bishop Dunstan. The rich and beautiful gifts both for himself and for his monastery of Fleury, which the monks and the bishops presented to him as he left them, indicate the magnitude of the indebtedness they felt for the assistance of this great teacher.

The letter of his abbot, Oylboldus (393), that summoned Abbo back to France is full of assurances that he is eagerly awaited by young and old, but especially by those who had some experience of his remarkable teaching. It is not strange, then, that shortly after his return, Abbo, the "bright and shining light," was elected abbot by his community and his election was ratified by King Hugh Capet. He interpreted his new responsibilities as caring for the physical, spiritual, and intellectual needs of his monks. While exhorting them to prayer and to scholarly tasks, he himself let no time pass without reading, writing, or dictating. The school, which Abbo called the "workshop of learning" (390), was at its apogee as it attracted students from all over northern Europe. The abbey library was second to no other in France, for it had most of the books basic to the teaching of the seven liberal arts and theology as well as many of the works of the Christian poets and most of the Latin classics. Although there is insufficient evidence to reconstruct the holdings of the library, from the abundance and variety of references in Abbo's works, it is obvious that they were remarkably extensive.[9] Associated with the library was a scriptorium where a distinctive style of writing was developed. Apparently the services of the scriptorium were solicited by scholars from other monasteries. Gerbert, for example, in 986 wrote to Constantine, who was then serving as schoolmaster at Fleury, asking him to supply him with copies of several works of Cicero.[10] A letter to Dunstan written by an unidentified monk of Fleury begs that several books that had long been in England be returned, since a fire at Fleury had destroyed the only copies there.[11]

For Abbo it was unfortunate that little time for purely scholarly pursuits was available throughout the rest of his life. He speaks with keen regret of becoming involved in the anxieties of administrative obligations and of having to leave the tranquillity of the studies he loved so well and by which he felt he might be of usefulness to others. Furthermore, he became engaged in bitter struggles to defend the rights and interests of his monks and of his abbey. On several occasions he felt compelled to set himself against his superior, Arnold, bishop of Orléans. Eventually his position became untenable and he had to make his defence to King Hugh and his son, Robert, in a long letter, his *Apologeticus* (461-472).

Abbo's role in ecclesiastical politics included participation in the Council of St. Basle in 991, the Council of St. Denis in 993, and the Councils of Mouzon and of Rheims in 995. Three times he made the journey to Rome, once serving as ambassador of King Robert to Pope Gregory V. He acted as peacemaker to several monasteries where the monks were in rebellion against their superiors. Once, for example, he took the part of the canons of St. Martin of Tours against their archbishop. His work as reformer took him on journeys to various houses from the Loire to the Garonne and was brought to a tragic climax with his death as a martyr at the hands of some revolting Gascon monks at La Réole in 1004.

A dedicated teacher, Abbo was passionately devoted to instilling into his pupils the desire for knowledge and freely and eagerly imparting to them his own learning. The sincerity of his declaration that there was nothing in life more pleasant than to learn and to teach is demonstrated by what he wrote as well as by what is recorded of his concern for his pupils. Almost all of his extant writings, with the possible exception of some of his letters, are expository or instructional in nature. His *Epitome de XCI Romanorum Pontificum Vitis* (535-570), an abridgment of an earlier *Liber Pontificalis,* begun by Anastasius, librarian of the papal library, and added to by Flodoardus and Liutprand, would serve as an important reference book in ecclesiastical history for his monastery. In the interests of Church and king, and in view of the ignorance of bishops, Abbo wrote a *Collectio Canonum* (473-508), a series of clarifications of fifty-two topics of canon law, in which he cites the Bible, the Church Fathers, the *Novellae* of Justinian, the *Capitularies* of Charlemagne, and the acts of the various Church Councils. Addressed to the Kings Hugh and Robert, the *Collectio* must also be considered in the nature of guide book to the duties and privileges of kings, bishops, and monks.

Many of his letters (419-452) contain instructional material; for example, to Odilo, abbot of Cluny, he wrote on the synoptic tables of the Gospels, "in the manner of a commentator," which he hoped would be pleasing to his friends and useful to later generations (425-429). He explains the system of numbering which occurs on the manuscripts of the Gospels, a phenomenon referring to the tables popularized by the canons of Eusebius in the fourth century. In order to make clear his explanation, he takes one example, the passage on the preaching and baptism of John the Baptist. He quotes the text of the four Gospels and indicates how the material is distributed unevenly in the four. He refers his readers to St. Augustine's *Harmony of the Gospels*.[12] Another letter, the tenth (433-436), to an unidentified bishop, is a treatise on taking an oath.[13] He develops his thesis there by discussing the nature of oath and the meaning of perjury. The whole letter is a good demonstration of Abbo's skill in dialectical exposition. Another letter (397-401) is an answer to a request from his pupil, Bernard, for advice when he was offered a bishopric for a rather large price, and the letter constitutes a clear treatment of the sin of simony.

Some of his didactic writings have been lost. He tells, for example, that once when he was a very young student in Paris, he heard a preacher announce in his sermon that Antichrist would come in the year one thousand and that the Last Judgment would follow (471). This heresy Abbo vigorously refuted, quoting the Gospels and the books of Daniel and Revelation. Several years later, after his return to Fleury, his abbot, Richard, asked him to reply to some men of Lorraine who had consulted him about the wide-spread belief that the world would come to an end when Good Friday fell on the date of the Annunciation, that is, in 970.

From Abbo's pen there are also purely didactic works in the fields of grammar, dialectic, and the mathematical arts. For his English brothers at Ramsey, in response to their questions, for the love he bore them, and in thankfulness for his escape from death at sea when coming to England, as well as to alleviate his own homesickness by doing something useful for his benefactors, he wrote a short treatise on grammatical topics, the *Quaestiones grammaticales* (521-534).[14] The monks had asked him several questions on the pronunciation of Latin words, about the length of vowels and accent. Abbo replied by citing the elementary rules set down by Donatus, then by quoting the grammarians, Priscian and Martianus Capella. Chiefly he answers the question by giving abundant examples of individual words and illustrations of their use by the Latin poets. During the course of his explanations, he reviews the rules of prosody. He explains the logic behind what seem to be irregularities in spelling in Latin. He discusses the transliteration of Greek words and warns against reproducing the Greek "x" by the Roman "x" instead of "ch." In a very interesting passage[15] he indicates that, unlike the Latin language, the Old English language of his hearers has a letter " þ " (thorn) which is the equivalent of the Greek " θ " (theta), and another letter " ƿ " (wen) which equals the old Greek digamma. With generous illustrations he discusses irregularities of Latin verbs and nouns, always with examples from the Latin authors. He explains an apparent grammatical error in the book of Maccabees (532). Two other points that Abbo mentions in his treatise are often cited for their theological context. He notes a grammatical error in the *Te Deum*, ascribed to St. Hilary of Poitiers, as it is commonly sung (532). Again he insists upon the orthodox reading of the phrase *Spiritus Sanctus—nec genitus, sed procedens* of the Athanasian Creed, as against the frequently used phrase—*nec ingenitus sed tantum procedens* (532). After some further information on miscellaneous subjects such as numbers and weights, he brings his work to a close in a light vein, expressing the hope that he has not bored his readers. Obviously this work on grammar is neither an elementary nor a systematic treatment so that one cannot judge properly the extent of his knowledge or his method of teaching it.

We are even less fortunate in his works on dialectic. His biographer assures us that he acquired complete mastery of the subject (390). Aristotle's logic was known in Europe in the tenth century through Boethius' commentaries on the *Categoriae*, the *Analytica*, and the *Topica*. These treatises Abbo studied with great interest and, while still a young man, wrote two works, one on hypothetical syllogisms and the other on categorical syllogisms and dedicated them to his pupil, Bernard. These works have only recently been identified in several tenth- and eleventh-century manuscripts but they have not been published.[16]

Abbo's works in the disciplines of the quadrivium fall into the categories of astronomy and arithmetic. Of these treatises some have not survived and, again, others have not been published. His biographer (390) states that he composed for the enlightenment of posterity several works on the revolution of the sun, of the moon, and of the planets. Only recently identified in manuscript, they, too, have not yet been published.[17] For his pupils he composed a catalogue of stars, which he appended to the treatise of Hyginus, and a short work on astronomy, which he added to the *Computus* of Helperic of Auxerre. While he was in England he wrote two more short treatises on astronomy.[18]

Abbo's English pupil, Byrhtferth, testifies to his teacher's skill in the art of teaching and his fund of information in arithmetic,[19] when he quotes from Abbo's account of the number 'ten.' Abbo himself, at the end of the *Quaestiones grammaticales* (534) refers to his commentary on the *Calculus* of Victorius of Aquitaine, a work on practical arithmetic, which consists of an introduction and a series of tables for the multiplication and division of numbers and fractions. In Abbo's commentary,[20] written at the urgent request of the monks of Fleury, he takes occasion to discuss the theory of numbers and their metaphysical properties, as well as to go into digressions on philosophy, astronomy, and physics, with a remarkable display of classical allusions. In the introduction (567-572) he indicates that in the interest of clarifying his subject he will add a good deal of material to his principal as he attempts to build a bridge to arithmetic which underlies all of the sciences and is of great usefulness for all kinds of practical purposes. This very important work, still largely unpublished, was of great interest in the Middle Ages for the use of fractions and for the rules for the use of the abacus. Of special note is his explanation of the various symbols which were used to designate fractions. He also explains certain confusing abbreviations and symbols used in the manuscripts.[21] Unlike the general run of commentaries which tend to consist of glosses on individual words or phrases of the principal, this commentary was written in continuous form with an occasional quotation from Victorius so that it gives the impression of an independent treatise.

Much of Abbo's work in the mathematical sciences was directed to the practical problem of the determination of the Christian calendar. In order to correct certain errors of calculation in the accepted calendar, based on the cycles of Dionysius, Abbo wrote a *Liber de computo* (390), only parts of which have been published.[22] It consists of a perpetual calendar, a series of tables marking the golden letters, and the seven lunar letters.[23] In addition to the various tables, there is an explanatory commentary, and finally, some information on astronomy. The second part also contains tables[24] and a criticism of the cycles of Dionysius. Towards the end of his life, Abbo again took up the subject of the errors in the Dionysian calculations in two letters written at the request of two of his pupils, Gerard and Vitalis. In these he explains the origin of the Dionysian cycles, their use by Bede, and the way they must be corrected to be accurate for his time.[25]

One can derive some impression of Abbo's status among

scholars by his association with the leading intellectuals of his day. Although the great Gerbert of Aurillac, later Pope Sylvester II, was often involved in political and ecclesiastical struggles and found himself bitterly opposed to Abbo, yet the two had respect for each other, and Abbo says (420) that in spite of their political differences he has always cherished and will continue to cherish Gerbert as a friend. Abbo's correspondents included Odilo, abbot of Cluny (425-429), Letaldus of Micy (438), Dunstan, archbishop of Canterbury,[26] and the brilliant schoolmaster and scholar, Fulbert, bishop of Chartres, who addressed him as, "O sacer abbas et magne philosophe."[27]

From the achievements in education and scholarship of his pupils, one can get some estimate of the effectiveness of Abbo as a teacher as one can also gauge his personal influence by the tributes paid him by these pupils. Aimoin, the biographer, is the best exemplar of this. A monk of Fleury throughout his life, Aimoin gave his full devotion to his abbot, his abbey, and his patron saint, St. Benedict. Throughout the biography his personal admiration for Abbo, whom he calls "most blessed father," can be felt. In turn, Abbo must have had great respect and affection for him since Aimoin accompanied his abbot on many of his missions and was with him at the time of his death at La Réole. Aimoin's literary career began when at Abbo's suggestion he wrote a *Historia Francorum*. His account of the abbots of Fleury has not survived. He composed a poetic version of the *Translatio S. Benedicti,* a continuation of the *Miracles of St. Benedict,* and a long *Sermon on St. Benedict.*[28] Aimoin wrote the biography of Abbo at the request of his fellow pupil, Herveus, later treasurer of St. Martin of Tours. He testifies that Herveus was devoted to Abbo and that Abbo loved him.[29]

From Abbo's own words, one concludes that the pupil to whom he felt the closest ties was Bernard, later abbot of Beaulieu and then bishop of Cahors.[30] When Abbo was far away, "exiled" in England, he spoke most poignantly of the sadness at the separation from his spiritual son, an association dearer to him than life itself

(523). When Bernard, disgusted with the world, applied for permission to make a pilgrimage to the Holy Land, Abbo refused to let him make the dangerous journey, but instead he sent him to Rome with several other monks (387-392).

The high tribute of Odolric, abbot of St. Martial of Limoges, has already been cited.[31] Another pupil was Constantine,[32] who became head of the Fleury school in 986 and later abbot of St. Mesmin of Micy. A good friend of Gerbert, he was teacher, poet, and musician. Another pupil of Abbo was Gauzlin, the natural son of King Hugh Capet, who succeeded Abbo as abbot of Fleury and saw to it that the school maintained its high position.[33] It was he who rebuilt the abbey of Fleury after it was burned in 1026. Later he became archbishop of Bourges. In England one distinguished teacher, Byrhtferth, had been Abbo's pupil at Ramsey.[34] In Germany two of Abbo's disciples gained some measure of fame: Berno,[35] who left Fleury to teach at Prüm and later became abbot of Reichenau, as a musician and liturgist, and Thierry of Fleury,[36] later of Amabach, as a hagiographer.

A full account of Abbo's heroic death which won for him the martyr's crown is given by his devoted biographer (409-411),[37] but one detail seems particularly pertinent to a consideration of the scholarly activities of the saint. With a number of monks from Fleury Abbo had come to the monastery at La Réole, then known as Squirs, to restore the disorganized and rebellious house to the observance of the Benedictine Rule, but his efforts met with great resistance from the belligerent Gascon monks. One day as he was at work on his books in the cloister, a noisy conflict broke out in the courtyard. With the intention of quieting the unruly mob, Abbo went out, still holding his pen and notebooks. Almost instantly one of the Gascons struck him in the side with a lance, mortally wounding him.

It would be interesting to know what piece of literary work was engaging the attention of Abbo during those tense days at La Réole. A manuscript now in the library of St. Gall may possibly furnish the answer.[38] The text of the manuscript is the anonymous life of St. Dunstan and the first folio contains a letter written about 1003 by Wulfric, abbot of Canterbury, to Abbo, stating that he is sending to him the prose biography of St. Dunstan with the earnest petition that he compose a poetic version. At the end of the manuscript there are several letters and charters showing that the manuscript early belonged to the monastery of Squirs. Thus circumstantial evidence makes it not improbable that at the time of his death, Abbo, like a good student, was at work on his last assignment, the life of his revered old friend, Dunstan of Canterbury.

V

Byrhtferth of Ramsey
(ca. 960- ca. 1012)

*Those who refuse to know and those who refuse to teach will be alike
guilty in the sight of the just Judge.*[1]

THE UNNAMED AUTHOR of the oldest and best biography of St.
Oswald[2] was a devout priest who had great admiration for
Oswald and deep reverence for the memory of Dunstan. He knew
the abbey of Ramsey very well; he gives a vivid description of the
countryside and quotes Abbo's poem on it; he names the buildings
and notes some of the special religious celebrations held there. His
references to Abbo of Fleury, whom he calls "philosopher" and
"that most worthy flower of the abbey of flowers," together with
his quotation of the two acrostic poems to Dunstan composed by
Abbo seem like the tributes of a student to his master. Justifiably
proud of his knowledge of classical authors, he often finds
occasion to allude to them, though less frequently than to the
Bible and works on theology. He shows considerable knowledge
of science, particularly of astronomy as he describes the heavenly
bodies and explains their courses in the sky. Unquestionably the
author was an Anglo-Saxon who favored "the efflorescent
rhetorical style"[3] characteristic of Aldhelm and others who were
influenced by the Irish teachers. Uncommon words, rather stilted
phrases, and an abundance of extended metaphors and similes
occur throughout. Many of these same words, phrases, and even
the figures of speech, not to mention echoes and parallels in
wording and phrasing and formulae of transition, are also found in

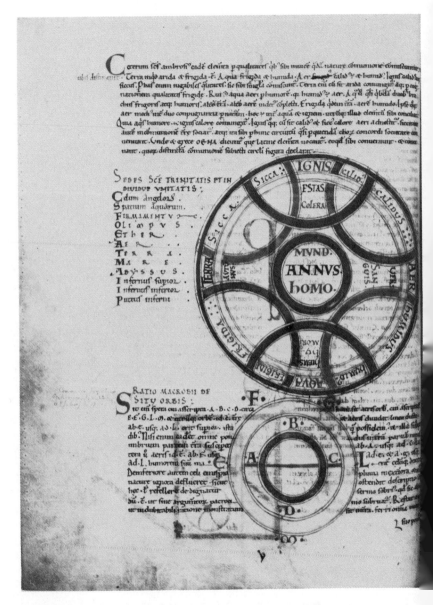

5. Byrhtferth's diagram of man and his world

Byrhtferth's *Manual.* All of this, particularly in view of the absence of any rival claimant, makes it altogether probable that the author of the *Vita Oswaldi* was Byrhtferth.[4]

There is no biography of Byrhtferth to furnish facts about the family, education, career, or writings of this notable schoolmaster who has been called "the most eminent man of science produced by the English Church since the death of Bede."[5] He must be judged solely upon the information he provides in his *Manual*, the only work which has been accepted as genuine by all scholars. It would seem that he came to the abbey of Ramsey as a young boy and received all of his education there. It was a fortunate chance that he was studying at Ramsey at the time when Abbo came to teach. Byrhtferth testifies both to Abbo's excellence when he calls him a "wise scholar" (57), "skilled in the art of teaching and proficient in learning" (233), and "learned teacher" (246), and also to specific facts and methods he learned from Abbo. Apparently Byrhtferth loved the abbey and remained there to teach for the rest of his life.

Byrhtferth's *Manual*, or *Enchiridion* as he calls it (133), written about 1011, is a handbook directed chiefly toward the secular priests who had not the benefit of the good training in Latin and the grounding in the liberal arts of the regular monks. It is essentially a *computus* mainly based upon three works of Bede, the *De temporibus*, *De temporum ratione*, and *De natura rerum*, and containing the fundamental elements of arithmetic and astronomy necessary for an understanding of the determination of the year and the establishment of the calendar. This information is generously illustrated by charts and diagrams of such phenomena as the signs of the zodiac, the twelve months, the solstices, equinoxes, the four elements, the four criteria for reckoning Easter, the Paschal cycle, the phases of the moon, and the lunar cycles. The most significant of these illustrations is a large diagram of the physical and physiological 'fours' where, within a great framework of the twelve months and the twelve signs of the zodiac, the main features are the two solstices and the two equinoxes and the four seasons of the year, the four points of the compass, the four cardinal winds, the four elements, the four ages of man, and the four mystic letters in the name of Adam, the first man. The diagram demonstrates the interrelation of the microcosm and the macrocosm, that is, the interdependence of man and his world, a theory that was to play a large role throughout medieval times.[6] The *Manual* also contains short treatises on rhetorical and grammatical subjects, as well as a treatment of diacritical marks used in texts, a table of weights and measures, an explanation of the numerical values traditionally assigned to the letters of the Greek, Latin, and Hebrew alphabets, and an extensive discourse on number symbolism. Also included are three theological tracts on the ages of the world, the loosing of Satan, and the eight capital sins. Appended are a brief *Ammonitio Amici* or *Friendly Advice* and a *Proemium* or *Preface* which appears to be in the nature of an epilogue, and may have been the conclusion of the *Manual*.[7] Byrhtferth begins his *Manual* in Latin; then, after a long paragraph, he gives a free translation of the same in English, saying that it is for the benefit of those who are unable to understand Latin (59). The system of alternating Latin and the vernacular translation continues for some space, but eventually the author uses English exclusively though he says that he is forced occasionally to intersperse Latin with the English because of the lack of technical terms (113). The long treatise on number symbolism is presented only in Latin.

Without question this unconventional book was compiled by Byrhtferth. He names himself several times, most significantly when he says (157), "In this present year, when Byrhtferth the author was writing this, there are fourteen epacts, and January has nine regulars," which dates the writing to the year 1011.[8] Again the author mentions the blessings he found at Ramsey "by the merciful grace of God,'' (15) and speaks of St. Oswald, in whom "the spirit of the fear of the Lord was gloriously displayed for our day." (213). On three occasions he cites the authority of Abbo, "skilled in the art of teaching and proficient in learning" (233), and even quotes what he used to say in class (57,233). As further sources for his own students to follow, he names Abbo (246), Bede (41,45,73,75,181,244), Isidore of Seville (189), Heiric of Auxerre (246), and Rhabanus Maurus (73).

The *Manual* was apparently designed as a utilitarian handbook, yet it has several features which the author thought more appropriate to poetry. There are, for instance, five invocations, none of them at the beginning of the work. Two are simple Latin quatrains asking the Holy Spirit to bestow the gift of language upon the writer (135,151); one (49-51) in a sustained metaphor represents the author sitting beside the vineyard in which he is about to labor, asking "the Son of the great David" to open his sight so that he may perform his task of explaining the calendar without error. The most elaborate (149) is a rough paraphrase of the preface of Aldhelm's *De Virginitate*,[9] where he bids the pagan Muses and Apollo depart, "and I trust that the glorious cherubim will come to me, and with his golden tongs bring to my tongue from off the heavenly altar a spark of the burning coal and touch the nerves of my dumb mouth" to give him the power of speech to translate the Paschal cycle into English. The last reveals the teacher (205) as he says, "May the grace of divine light deign to illumine my poor mind—so great is my desire to convey all in my power to mortals in this brief work." Images of light, fire, and radiance appear throughout, but some rather unusual figures are used in several passages where Byrhtferth considers his own mission as a teacher. "The broody hen," he says, "though she cluck piteously, often spreads out her wings and keeps the chickens warm; in the same way, it is our intention to solace our youths with this teaching." (79). Again he remarks, "We have stirred with our oars the waves of the deep pool; we have likewise beheld the mountains around the salt sea strand. . . . The waves symbolize this profound art, and the mountains, too, symbolize the magnitude of this art." (15)

Byrhtferth reveals himself consistently as a sympathetic teacher, ever alert and sensitive to his hearers, as he addresses them as "amiable brother" or "gracious learner." One gets the impression, however, that some of his pupils were rather reluctant, but their aversion to learning only presented a challenge to the master. Once he says (59), "I began in my heart to ruminate by what remedy I might help clerks to relax their dice-playing, and obtain a knowledge of this art (of computation). Above I applied to them a fairly large poultice; now I want to administer to them a draught also." Again he remarks (17), "We know of a surety that there are very many rustic clerks who do not know how many kinds of years (that is solar, lunar, and a decennovennal or year of the nineteen-year cycle) there are; but I am willing to show myself indulgent to their slothfulness." Yet he makes clear to them their responsibility for learning, when he says (59), "Since what we have just said is suited to lazy clerks, saving their reverence, we admonish them to learn those things of which they are ignorant, and afterwards to teach others what they have learned. Those who refuse to know and those who refuse to teach, will be alike guilty in the sight of the just Judge. Both therefore receive the same punishment. Let this stern reproof of ours suffice at present." Not solely the lazy clerks but also the country priests who had no opportunity for learning are his concern, for he says, (194), "We will next reveal to country priests the mysteries of the letters of the alphabet." Again, he observes (117), "I expect, O rustic priest, that thou dost not know what an 'atom' is." The knowledge that he offers will save the priests from embarrassment before their bishops, as he exhorts them (37), "Now I would that the noble clerks shook off all sloth from their mind and intellect in order that they might be able the more excellently to give an account of the epacts in the presence of reverend bishops." The master, too, had his own reputation to protect, as he indicates (191), "It seems to me necessary that I should explain this method of reckoning sufficiently to priests so that I shall not be ashamed when well-educated men hear this treatise."

It has been suggested that the *Manual* represents the teacher's lecture notes, for his exposition is constantly interrupted by direct address to the listeners, sometimes by way of encouragement or even flattery. Perhaps this mannerism may be explained by the fact that the teacher was endeavoring to elucidate a rather complex subject to an audience of widely differing backgrounds and training which included clerks, rustic priests, young monks who had been studying since their childhood, and also young boys. To the latter he shows himself most tactful as he suggests that the material is difficult and that, indeed, he himself as a boy in school was once "exposed to a very fiery trial before we succeeded in investigating these mysteries" (95). To the more able students he suggests sources for further reading (73,227). He apologizes for the necessarily elementary nature of his own exposition when he says, (133), "We implore scholars and educated men, who know these things perfectly, not to be annoyed with these things which in our imperfect fashion we set down and serve up to young boys."

In expounding to his heterogeneous audience the "mysteries" of the great divisions of time and the astronomical methods for determining the Christian calendar, Byrhtferth used very simple pedagogical methods. Every familiar device for enlisting and holding the attention of the hearer is used. These can be noted in his varied opening sentences: "We shall now explain—," "I want to show the origin—," "Let us now turn our attention—," "Note, if you please—," "Why is it, O brother, that thou makest the moon to be the same age in the first of April and the first of May?" "What need is there for so often adding thirty?" Surely his most effective teaching aid was the diagram, which he used very frequently. "We will first inscribe here the zodiac circle with the names of the twelve signs and the appellations of the twelve months, that our reader may have what we are talking about before his eyes (7-9)." "O amiable brother, notice carefully this wheel; it will show thee very clearly the whole course of the moon (163)." "The number one thousand is a perfect number as is also clearly shown by the following diagram (233)." It would appear that he had some sense of fun when he said, (19) "Each year (to tell you a secret) there will be a solar year and a lunar year, and likewise a decennovennal year." Again he says (71) "Understand, young man, when I now whisper in thy ear." He is also showing a touch of humor when he says (165), "When thou, O reverend brother, hearest that the moon is twelve spaces from the sun, then do thou understand that, as if I were to say: 'Byrhtferth the priest stands or sits in the twelfth place after Bishop Eadnoth.'"

It is unfortunate that the stature of Byrhtferth as a teacher should have to be judged solely by the incidental directions and advice provided in the *Manual* of information necessary for monks and priests, for surely his performance in instructing his pupils could be accurately measured only by his oral presentation. Not even his own knowledge of the mathematical sciences can really be determined, as one notes that he apologizes several times for having to present only elementary material. Further, no other works of his on the arts or sciences have survived, though two are mentioned: *De principiis mathematicis* and *De institutione mona-chorum*.[10] Glosses on four technical treatises by Bede which older biographers attributed to Byrhtferth have now been shown to be earlier than his time.[11] Also the life of Dunstan written by a certain "Presbyter B" was long considered the work of By-rhtferth, but this attribution has now been shown unlikely.[12] In spite of these limitations, it does seem safe to say that Byrhtferth was properly trained for his work, that he undertook his assignment with determination to succeed, and that his very understanding of his students and his sympathy for their inadequate backgrounds insured some degree of success.

Although Byrhtferth must have trained some of his students to such proficiency that they were able to succeed him in the direction of the school at Ramsey, no record of this has been preserved. Only one incident mentioned in the history of the abbey written by a monk a generation later gives an indication of the character of the school in Byrhtferth's day and the later careers of some of his pupils. We learn that four young boys, sons of distinguished families, who had been sponsored initially by Bishop Oswald and had been in the abbey since their early childhood, used to go outside the cloister for recreation at specified times with the permission of their master. One day they went for a walk and happened to notice the ropes of the great bells hanging from the west tower of the church, perhaps the very bells that had been presented to the new abbey by King Edgar.[13] Of course, the boys rang the bells and so vigorously and inexpertly that one of them was badly cracked and rendered discordant. When the misdemeanor became known, the monks demanded that the culprits be severely whipped. Only the kind-hearted abbot was able to regard the misdeed as a youthful prank, the result of thoughtlessness rather than malice. He managed, with difficulty, to calm the wrath of the community and then to admonish the wrong-doers in private and to give them a suitable penance. Later in the *History* three of the principals of the episode appear again. Ethericus, grown wise and understanding, became bishop of Dorchester. He often visited Ramsey and endowed it with many rich gifts in gratitude for the forebearance of his old abbot, and with the support of King Canute had the bones of St. Felix, first bishop of the East Angles, transferred to Ramsey as a kind of reparation for the damage to the bells. He was succeeded as bishop of Dorchester by his old schoolmate, Ednotus. Like Ethericus, Ednotus loved Ramsey and for his part in the youthful prank gave the abbey three large tracts of land. The two bishops were buried in Ramsey. The third of the youthful bellringers, Oswald, nephew of Bishop Oswald, showed such scholarly interests and religious devotion that his uncle sent him to Fleury to complete his education in the seven liberal arts and to experience the life at that distinguished monastery. There he made great progress in his studies and became a friend of Constantine. Upon his return to England, it is said that he was offered a bishopric but he declined it, asking to remain in his beloved Ramsey to devote his life to study. It would seem very unusual if this learned monk was not assigned the responsibility of teaching to carry on the tradition of Abbo and Byrhtferth.

6. Miniature from Aelfric's translation of Genesis: Abraham sacrificing Isaac

VI

Aelfric of Eynsham
(ca. 955 - ca. 1010)

*It befits teachers that they salt the minds of believing men
with the salt of wisdom.*[1]

AELFRIC, the one-time pupil of Bishop Ethelwold and later his
biographer, has been given the epithet "Grammaticus" or "The
Teacher" to differentiate him from many other men of his
generation known by the same name. This designation was most
appropriate, for he was preeminently the teacher,[2] first as he
wrote sermons for laymen and translated large sections of the
Bible for them, then as he provided theological information to
priests and even to bishops, and finally as he instructed young
oblates and monks in his abbey.

What little is known of the life of Aelfric has been gathered
from incidental references in the prefaces to his various writings.
He seems to have been born of a middle-class family in Wessex
about 955. His introduction to learning came from a local priest
who undertook to teach him Latin, though he himself could
scarcely understand the language and was so lacking in theology
that he did not know the difference between the Law of the Old
Testament and that of the New.[3] Sometime after 970 Aelfric was
sent to the monastic school at Winchester where he learned the
discipline of the Benedictine Rule. There he also received
instruction in the liberal arts, in theology and patristic literature,
and in Church history from the monks and on occasion from
Ethelwold himself.[4] The firm but gentle manner of the bishop in

teaching his pupils made such a great impression on Aelfric that it influenced his whole philosophy of education. After his student days he remained as priest at Winchester for many years, gaining the wide knowledge which later won for him the reputation of being "probably the best-educated man in the England of his day."[5] Undoubtedly during this time he was also called upon to teach.

In 987 Aelfric was sent by his bishop to a new monastery recently founded in Dorset, at Cernel, by an influential nobleman, Aethelmaer, in order to institute the Benedictine Rule there and to supervise the school. With the assumption of this new responsibility, Aelfric seems to have gained a fresh understanding of his role as teacher and to have experienced a deep dedication to his vocation, so that everything he did or wrote thereafter was directed toward the instruction of those who were not in possession of the knowledge that he had. From his own words we learn that he considered himself in a kind of apostolic succession of teachers: "Our Lord commanded his disciples that they should instruct and teach all people the things which he himself taught to them; but of those there are too few who will well teach and well exemplify. . . . From such commands it appeared to me that I should not be guiltless before God, if I would not declare to other men, by tongue or by writings, the evangelical truth, which he himself spoke, and afterwards to holy teachers revealed."[6]

During the eighteen years spent at Cernel, Aelfric demonstrated the sincerity of his convictions as he composed numerous works intended for the instruction of laymen in their Christian heritage, for the education of the clergy in the performance of their priestly obligations, and for young pupils to give them a basic training in Latin. In 1005 he went as abbot to the new monastery of Eynsham in Oxfordshire, also founded by Aethelmaer. Besides establishing the new community in the way of the Benedictine Rule and overseeing the varied activities of the new house, Aelfric wrote a number of letters on doctrinal questions. His life of St. Ethelwold was also written during these years. The date of

Aelfric's death is not recorded, but there is no indication of his work after 1010.

Although he spent most of his life as a simple priest in one small abbey, Aelfric had the greatness of mind to outline for himself and then carry out a long-range plan for restoring Christian learning to his country. His first and lasting concern was for the laity who were for the most part ignorant of the fundamentals of Christian history, theology, and ethic. Furthermore, many were indifferent or even hostile toward learning and had no interest in adopting a new way of life. Moreover, those who had some interest in learning had access to very few books in English and some of these books contained false doctrine which the unlearned had no way of judging. Therefore, for the edification of these people and to exhort them to virtuous lives, Aelfric composed in English two series of forty sermons each, appropriate for the Sundays and feast days of the Christian year, to be read by the priests to their people. These *Catholic Homilies*,[7] all instructional in intent, some exegetical and Scriptural, some a mingling of legendary and historical accounts of the lives of the saints, were derived largely from the writings of the Fathers. They supply information concerning Christian world history from the Creation, through the Incarnation, to the Last Judgment; they provide doctrinal instruction from the teachings of Christ and their interpretation by the Fathers; they present witnesses to the Faith in the lives of the saints; and they provide moral instruction to insure salvation.

In the Latin prefaces to these *Homilies,* as well as in the English sermons themselves, the teacher reveals his attitude toward his potential hearers and his method for enlisting their attention. Introducing the first series, he says, "However rashly or presumptuously undertaken, I have nevertheless formed this book out of Latin writers, and from Holy Scripture, translating into our ordinary speech, for the edification of the simple, who know only this language both for reading and for hearing; and for that reason I have used no difficult words, but only plain English; so that our message might the more readily reach the hearts of those who read or hear, to the profit of the souls of those who cannot be taught in any other tongue than that to which they are born."[8] In his attempt to adapt his material to his audience, he avoids pedantry: " . . . I have not everywhere translated word for word, but have given the sense; and at the same time have carefully avoided falling into errors that might lead astray, lest I should be found carried away with any heresy, or darkened by any fallacy."[9] Simplicity and brevity seemed necessary for his purpose. "One should speak to laymen according to the measure of their understanding, so that they be not disheartened by the deepness, nor by the length wearied."[10] Yet Aelfric was tactful toward his untutored hearers, as he suggests that some subjects are difficult even for the educated. Speaking of the inner meaning of the experience of Job, for example, he says, "For the deepness of the narrative transcends our understanding, and yet more that of the unlearned."[11] He felt a great urgency to provide whatever aids to salvation he could, since the tenth century was nearing its end and the Day of Judgment at hand. "Now ye require, laymen, great learning at this time, because this world is greatly afflicted through manifold troubles, and as the end of this world is nearer, so is the persecution of the devil greater. . . . Now need ye so much more the comfort of books."[12] To serve the very basic needs of these people, he also made English translations of the Pater noster, the Creed, and several of the more common prayers of the Church.[13] Ironically, in teaching in such a simple way, he had to risk his own reputation as a scholar. One sees this in the *Homilies* as he apologizes for abridging the Latin accounts in his translation,[14] and in his precise statement of his purpose in the final prayer: "I have disclosed these two books to the English race, for the unlearned; the learned have no need of these books, because their own learning may suffice them."[15] Both sets of *Homilies* had the sanction of the Church, as one sees since he dedicated them to Siguric, archbishop of Canterbury.

The clergy, too, often poorly educated because of the absence of schools and the earlier destruction of libraries, and frequently lacking any concept of the priestly ideal, were the objects of Aelfric's concern. On a number of occasions in the *Homilies* (which the priests were expected to read in their churches) he exhorts them to learn and to preach what they have learned. He asks, "How can the unlearned hold a teacher's authority, and aptly preach to the lay-folk? . . . Long shall he learn who is to teach, and have authority and obedience, lest he misguide the lay-folk with himself. That teacher has little authority, who with evil example makes void his preaching. He is a great teacher who preaches to men and also sets a good example by works."[16] Aelfric constantly reminds the priests that preachers are teachers who, as successors to the apostles, are under obligation to enlighten laymen by sharing their knowledge of God's plan for salvation. Speaking in the metaphorical language of the Bible, he says, "It befits the teachers that they salt the minds of believers with the salt of wisdom, so that whosoever shall approach them may be strewed over with the savour of the everlasting life."[17] How necessary such exhortations were can be judged from numerous references that Aelfric makes to the priests' failure to live up to their obligations. He speaks "with great sorrow" as he remarks, "Lo, now this world is filled with priests, but, nevertheless, in God's reaping few of them are working."[18] As one of the four things through which the souls of men perish, he names the "heedlessness of teachers" and says, "Over the teachers is God's ire most excited, because they neglect the divine books, and are wholly solicitous about worldly things."[19] He is more gentle with the unlettered priest as one sees when he says, "If the priest cannot say a homily to the lay-folk, he should, at least, through the innocence of his life, set them a good example."[20]

For the special edification of the clergy, Aelfric wrote in English a third series of forty homilies for the Christian year, usually known as the *Lives of the Saints*.[21] These narratives, translated largely from the Fathers, consist of the lives of the early martyrs, the confessors, and particularly the English saints[22] whom the clergy honored in special observances. Even from the priests, who in their ignorance might misunderstand and be led astray, he withheld some saints' lives, notably from the *Vitae patrum*.[23] One of these sermons, called *The Memory of the Saints*,[24] gives a general outline of the plan for the whole series. Aelfric lists the holy men of old, prophets and patriarchs and other good men whose lives were pleasing to God, all anticipating the glorious life of Christ. He then names the apostles and saints who followed Christ's teachings, some of whom gave their lives for their beliefs. Then he treats the eight deadly sins[25] which destroy men and the eight cardinal virtues by which these evils may be overcome. Throughout his sermons Aelfric stresses moral values. He expresses the hope that they "will refresh by their exhortations such as are slothful in the faith."[26] The intelligent priest, even the inadequately educated, would find in these homilies a great store of information on Church history and Christian doctrine.

Appended to the *Lives of the Saints* are two homilies, *On False Gods*[27] and *The Twelve Abuses*.[28] The first would indicate that the Church was still fighting against the superstitions of the ancient religion of Britain but more actively against the idolatrous practices of the Danish invaders, so that the priests needed some instruction for combatting them. The subject of *The Twelve Abuses,* the private evils that destroy society, had been touched upon in the *Lives,* but they are here spelled out for the priests.

For the practical purpose of giving the priests and monks some idea of the method for determining the Church calendar, particularly for establishing the date of Easter in any given year, Aelfric wrote *De temporibus anni,*[29] a short treatise in English, largely an adaptation and summary of the pertinent parts of Bede's standard works on the astronomical calculation of time and the determination of the calendar. Under Aelfric's hand this became a straightforward piece of expository prose, giving elementary instruction in astronomy, cosmology, and meteorology. Although it was intended for a reference book, "not for a sermon, but to be read by those whom it so pleaseth," it also bears the mark of the teacher. Aelfric makes the whole subject come alive by using the first person, by introducing contemporary references, by interjecting apostrophe and rhetorical questions, and by pointing out some commonly-held errors. The treatise bears witness to Aelfric's genuine interest in astronomy, an interest also shown by numerous references to it in his other works.

Even some of the bishops, it would seem, stood in need of exhortation from the schoolmaster. Aelfric has outlined their responsibilities in one of the homilies. "A bishop should constantly instruct his people with book-learning, and set them a good example, reprove the perverse, and love the virtuous, be a faithful shepherd under Christ, overseeing all, as his name indicates; and not conceal evil, nor consent to injustice."[30] At least two distinguished bishops recognized Aelfric's talents and applied to him to prepare official communications for their clergy. For one of these, Wulfsige of Sherborne, Aelfric composed a pastoral letter for the priests of his diocese. This lengthy canon, known as the *Letter for Wulfsige,*[31] and written in the bishop's name, in English, defines in detail the rules of conduct for the priests, their pastoral duties, and their responsibilities to the laymen. About one-third of the letter is concerned with the very heart of the Christian ritual, the Eucharist, as he explains the nature of the sacrament, the manner of administering it, and the special circumstances of its celebration on feast days. Throughout the treatise Aelfric repeatedly emphasizes the function of the priest as teacher. He says, for example, "Let the teacher warn against that which the prophet says, 'Canes muti non possunt latrare.' 'Dumb dogs cannot bark.' We ought to bark and preach to the laymen, lest, for want of instruction, they should perish."[32] A rather stern Latin letter to Wulfsige precedes the canon. In it Aelfric observes that it would be inappropriate for him to outline the duties of the bishop to his priests, but he continues, "I say, nevertheless, those things which you ought again and again to say to your clergy, and in regard to which should show their remissness, since through their frowardness the canon laws, and the religion and doctrine of holy church are destroyed. Free your mind, therefore, and tell them what ought to be regarded by the priests and ministers of Christ, lest you yourself perish likewise, if you are accounted a dumb dog."[33]

Two more long pastoral letters written at the request of Wulfstan, archbishop of York and bishop of Worcester, first in Latin and then translated into English, also outline the duties and obligations of priests. A large part of the text is concerned with a summary of world history as it relates to Church history and the Christian experience. The second letter also includes instructions for the proper celebration of the Mass on the important feast days, and a discussion of the Ten Commandments and the eight deadly sins. Here, again, Aelfric insists upon the necessity for learning by the teacher-preacher. "Long should he learn who has to teach; and if he will not learn to be a teacher of right wisdom, he shall afterwards be a teacher of great error. Blind is the guide, who has to teach God's folk, if he have neither learning, nor is willing to learn, but misleads himself, and his parishioners along with him."[34]

Aelfric's first official act after he was called to become abbot at Eynsham was to provide a *De consuetudine monachorum,* an abridgment and English translation of Ethelwold's *Regularis Concordia* for the guidance of the monks in the new monastery.[35] In a Latin letter addressed to the monks as a preface, he tells them that he feels it his duty to instruct them in monastic usage since they are new to the religious life. Even so, he is timid about presuming to do this and hesitant to tell them all the things he himself learned in Ethelwold's school for fear they may be discouraged by the strictness of these observances, and so gives only the essentials of monastic usage.

During those first busy years at Eynsham, Aelfric also wrote a life of St. Ethelwold[36] as a personal tribute to his teacher and a memorial to his achievements. Addressed to Bishop Kenulph and the monks at Winchester, it must have been written with the further objective of setting before the brothers the noble example of devotion and piety of that great bishop.

Very appropriately and wholly in keeping with his character, Aelfric prepared for his monks an English translation of St. Basil's charming *Advice to a Spiritual Son*.[37] The original treatise of the fourth-century Greek Father who was greatly concerned with monastic discipline has been lost, but a Latin translation, probably made by Rufinus in the sixth century, was long associated with the Rule of St. Benedict. It is this work (only half of which is extant) that Aelfric undertook to make available to his community. It does not outline the duties of the monks but rather touches upon such questions as spiritual warfare, the virtue of the soul, love of God, love for one's neighbor, the desire for peace and charity, on avoiding the love of the world, and on shunning avarice. In his prologue the words Aelfric ascribes to St. Basil surely come from his own heart as he addresses his own beloved spiritual sons. "Hear thou, my child, the admonition of thy father, and incline now thine ear to my words, and with a believing heart listen to what I say; I wish to tell thee, and truly to teach thee that spiritual labour, how thou mayest fight for God, and with what measure thou mightest serve Him. . . . These words are not from me, but from the instruction of God; I will not instruct thee now with a new doctrine, but with that doctrine which I learned of old, from the holy men that were our predecessors."[38]

For laymen, priests, bishops, and monks alike, Aelfric's translations from the Bible and his Biblical interpretations were of prime importance to his great educational plan. In the two series of *Catholic Homilies* which were intended to be followed throughout the Christian year, sections of Biblical text appear in Aelfric's translation as he gives the Scripture readings appointed for the various days. Further, some rather long quotations from the Bible occur by way of illustration in these sermons, most notably an entire sermon that consists of an extensive epitome-translation of the book of Job.[39] His *Lives of the Saints*, too, contains long paraphrase-translations of Kings[40] and Maccabees.[41] Like many of his contemporaries, Aelfric had grave misgivings about the propriety of translating Holy Scripture as he also realized the risk of misinterpretation by improperly educated priests who might then teach false doctrine, so he refused to translate the Gospels.[42] He was very hesitant about translating the Old Testament with its alien customs and unfamiliar laws which might be misunderstood and hence might lead people astray. Consequently he "edited" his text, omitting some parts, paraphrasing others, abbreviating in places, and in general adjusting it to the experience of his readers. He also indicated the spiritual interpretation of the passage and pointed out the moral teaching to be derived from it. The only independent Biblical translation Aelfric made was done at the request of Aethelweard who asked him to translate the book of Genesis. In his prefatory letter he says that he will translate only the first part since the second part has already been done, his translation now incorporated into what is known as *The Old English Heptateuch.*[43] In this rendition of the beginning of the Bible, Aelfric followed the original quite faithfully except that he omitted certain genealogies and other matters which he felt unsuitable or unnecessary, as he also compressed the narrative in some places, all in the interest of making it more comprehensible to the reader. Also credited to Aelfric are four comparable translations from Joshua,[44] Judges,[45] Esther,[46] and Judith,[47] perhaps made originally for homilies. Appended to the narrative of Judges, to make it more relevant to his readers, is an epilogue on the English kings who also "were often victorious through God," notably King Alfred, Athelstan, and "the noble and resolute" King Edgar who "exalted the praise of God everywhere among his people—and God subdued for him his adversaries."[48]

Aelfric himself may have felt that his most effective teaching of the truths of the Christian religion lay in his expositional works. His first effort in this field was an English translation of Alcuin's *Interrogationes Sigewulfi in Genesin* or *Queries of Sigewulf*[49] on the book of Genesis, which was originally appended to the *Lives of the Saints.* Here he presents the most significant of Alcuin's explanations of the main tenets of Christian doctrine as they are revealed in the Bible. His own more comprehensive and very logical treatment of the subject, written at the request of a prominent layman, is found in his *Letter for Sigeweard*, often entitled, *On the Old and New Testaments*.[50] This exposition of universal history as a demonstration of the working out of the divine plan provides just the kind of instruction that would be most useful for both clergy and laity. Here Aelfric takes up the books of the Bible in order, giving a summary of each, and explaining its place in the whole scheme of Christian theology. For him world history is an orderly progression from Creation, the Fall of Man, the Prophecies of the Old Testament, to the Incarnation, the Redemption, and the Final Judgment.

In two more theological treatises, Aelfric focuses upon rather restricted topics, but he demonstrates their wider importance in the Christian experience. The first is a translation-adaptation of St. Basil's *Hexameron*,[51] made from Eustathius' Latin translation, and it gives the account of the six days of Creation. Here he explains the physical beginning of life on earth, but his chief purpose is to relate it to God's plan for the redemption of the human race. The second is a sermon, *De septiformi spiritu* or the *Sevenfold Gifts of the Holy Spirit*.[52] As in his homily on Pentecost,[53] he begins with the prophecy of Isaiah concerning the coming of the Messiah upon whom the Spirit of the Lord will rest, then shows how the promise was fulfilled at the baptism of Christ when the Holy Spirit came down in the form of a dove and later to the disciples in the form of fire, and finally discusses the mystery in its relevance to men's lives in his own day.

Although Aelfric gave much time and thought to the instruction of the laity and the clergy, one must assume that his main occupation throughout his life was teaching the young boys and monks. Since these pupils would all be concerned in one way or another with the service of the Church and so would have to be familiar with the liturgy and the various offices, all of which were in Latin, it was imperative for them to know it thoroughly. It goes without saying that all higher education depended upon a firm foundation in the language. To fulfill this fundamental need,

Aelfric composed three works as aids to the teaching of Latin: the *Grammar, Glossary,* and *Colloquy.* They are of unusual interest because they give some impression of Aelfric's methods of teaching in the classroom; they are also important in revealing Aelfric's own knowledge of the language and his understanding of the relationship of Latin to English.

From his long experience in teaching, Aelfric realized that it was very difficult for young boys to learn Latin from the current textbooks, so he took the extraordinary step of translating Latin grammar into English, thus constructing what is considered the earliest Latin grammar in the vernacular in all of medieval Europe.[54] He defends this unusual procedure in his Latin preface: "I, Aelfric, as one of slight wisdom, have chosen these extracts from the smaller and from the larger work of Priscian, and have translated them into your own language for you little boys of tender years; that after having read through the eight parts of speech of Donatus, you may be able to receive both languages into your tender minds, while you progress toward higher studies."[55] Since he knows the conservatism and the snobbish exclusiveness of some of the educated toward the untutored, he adds that he will be the object of criticism, but that he is content to follow the teaching that he himself received at the school of Ethelwold. He continues, now in English, to say that grammar is the key that unlocks the meaning of books, and he hopes the boys will be assisted to higher scholarship through its help. He then gives the ultimate purpose of his work: "It behooves the servants of God and the monks to take heed lest holy learning grow cold and fail in our days, even as happened among the English only a few years ago."[56]

Aelfric, as he says, used the standard works of Priscian and Donatus for his *Grammar,* and as he also used Isidore of Seville's treatment of grammar in his *Etymologiae,* one cannot consider it a piece of simple translation, but rather a reorganization of the old presentations of the basic morphology of the Latin language and the syntax of Latin grammar. Aelfric begins with his own introduction, containing definitions of the concepts of 'voice,' 'letter,' 'syllable,' 'diphthong,' and a brief consideration of the eight parts of speech. The rest of the *Grammar* is a conventional treatment of the parts of speech: noun, pronoun, verb, adverb, participle, conjunction, preposition, and interjection. For each category he gives a definition, presents the English translation for the technical terms, names the groups into which they may be divided, and states the function and properties of the part of speech.

Some impression of the way in which the *Grammar* was presented is indicated by Aelfric's interpolations of explanatory phrases and directional hints. Departing from the stereotypes of Donatus and Priscian, he explains the specialized words in simple language and in sufficient detail to give the boys an insight into their nature and function. Furthermore, he gives abundant illustrations, often omitting the stock examples of the old grammarians and giving others adapted to the boys' experience. In explaining the noun, for instance, he cites *rex* and *episcopus, Eadgarus* and *Aethelwoldus* (8); to illustrate the adjective he mentions *romanus, anglus,* and *lundoniensis* (13); and to demonstrate cases, he uses the following pertinent examples: *hi pueri discunt, his pueris ministro, hos pueros flagello, ab his pueris doctus sum,* and *O pueri, cantate bene* (23). (Surely the boys must have been amused at the examples for the accusative, "I flog these boys" and for the ablative, "I am taught by these boys!") For examples of syntax, his illustrations are sufficiently extensive to give the boys a grasp of the composition, as for instance in the following: *Quis hoc fecit? Ego hoc feci. Quid das mihi? Unum librum do tibi. O magister, doce me aliquid. Ab hoc magistro audivi sapientiam. Docturus sum cras pueros* (22-23). Aelfric did not hesitate to omit or severely abbreviate some of the sections of Priscian where the details might be burdensome or inappropriate for the boys. As an example of this, in the section on swearing oaths (224), he says that the Romans used the preposition with the accusative of the noun, but since Christ forbade his followers to swear, there is no need of discussing the matter.

In teaching Latin, which all acknowledge as the indispensable tool for all scholarsihp, Aelfric never shows the slightest hint of patronage toward his native English language. To the contrary, in both introductions he states that the present work should be a help to the student of both Latin and English. Where it is appropriate, he makes comparisons between the structure and usages of the two languages. When speaking of the letters of the alphabet, for example, he says that although Latin did not originally have the letter 'y,' it appears in Latinized Greek words (5), but that this letter is commonly used in English. Again, in speaking of patronymics which are common in Greek but not generally used by the Romans, he notes that such words are frequently used in English, and he gives examples, such as *Pendingas* and *Cwicelmingas* (15). Aelfric did, however, have the problem of finding words to express some of the technical Latin grammatical terms. For the names of the very common classifications, such as *letter, verb,* and *tense,* he used the familiar English words, *staef* (4), *word* (119), and *tid* (123). For the more unusual terms, however, he had to coin words, as, for example, *interjectio* became *betwuxalegedrys* (between placing) (218), *praepositio* became *foresetnyss* (set before) (10), and *subjunctivus* became *underdeodendlic* (under-joining) (126).

As an ancilla to his Latin *Grammar,* Aelfric composed a *Glossary,*[57] a Latin-English vocabulary list of nouns and some adjectives for the use of his pupils in writing Latin sentences. This is not an alphabetical lexicon, as many of the medieval glossaries are, but words arranged in various groups, each centered around one subject or area of experience. These include the names of the Creator and the divisions of his creation, names of parts of the human body, members of society, occupations, the arts and sciences. It continues with names of birds, fish and monsters of the sea, names of wild and domestic animals, names of plants, vegetables, and flowers, names of trees, names of building materials, weapons, household utensils, and miscellaneous words that would be useful in ordinary conversation. Aelfric did not consider his list of some three thousand words comprehensive since, he says, that would be impossible. Certainly it was well suited to his purpose, for with the *Grammar* and the *Glossary* the boys had the means for learning to read Latin and to write it correctly, as well as to speak it. Most probably it also served some of the less experienced teachers.

Aelfric devised a third teaching aid for these *pueruli,* as he calls them, an exercise in conversation to give them facility in speaking and practice in correct pronunciation. This *Colloquium*[58] or *Conversation* is a humble and remote descendant of the dialogue which had such an honorable history in the wider educational process in Greece, and appeared as the diatribe in Hellenistic times, but it is a more direct imitation of a widely circulated Latin-Greek reader, the *Hermeneumata Pseudo-Dositheana,* centered around the *Grammar* of the fourth century Greek grammarian Dositheus, a book that had been used by several of Aelfric's predecessors.[59] Since Aelfric's purpose was to teach Latin, the book was written in Latin, but some later student or possibly a teacher furnished it with an interlinear gloss in English. This has led one critic to call it a "tutor's key" and to say that it represents "the earliest example of those wooden legs for halting teachers."[60] Rather than this, it was originally written without a gloss and devised as a model exercise for teaching by the direct method. As it appears in one of the best manuscripts (Cott. Tib. A.3) it has the Latin title which is translated as "A Colloquy for exercising boys in speaking Latin; first compiled by Aelfric, and added to by Aelfric Bata, his disciple." Bata seems to have enlarged his master's work by attaching some further dialogue of a rather pedantic nature.

One must imagine that the boys had access to the *Grammar* and the *Glossary* and that they were assigned specific groups of words on one topic upon which they could expect to be tested. To make learning more lively and amusing, the Master gave each boy the role of an artisan or laborer. In class he catechized them with questions entailing their use of words associated with the assumed role. For example, the Master asks the boy who is pretending to be a shepherd, "What do you say, Shepherd, have you any work?" The Shepherd replies, "Indeed, I have. In early morning I drive my sheep to the pastures, and I stand by them, in heat and cold, with dogs, lest the wolves should devour them, and I bring them back to their folds, and milk them twice a day, and I move their folds; besides I also make butter and cheese, and I am faithful to my lord." (184-185). Of the Shoemaker, the Master asks, "You, Shoemaker, what do you produce?" He answers, "My craft is indeed very useful and necessary for you." "How is that?" asks the Master. "I buy skins and hides, and prepare them, and make various kinds of sandals, slippers, shoes, and high boots, besides bridles, harness, and other horse trappings, halters and spurs; and also leather bottles, flasks, purses, and bags." (189) In the course of the conversation, the Master questions boys who impersonate a ploughboy, an oxherd, a huntsman, a fisherman, a fowler, a merchant, a salter, a baker, a cook, a blacksmith, and a woodman. Throughout the conversation, the Master speaks very little but gives the boys every opportunity to display their learning.

The *Colloquy* is not merely an exercise in vocabulary, but a means of affording practice in both composition and pronunciation, as one sees in the opening of the conversation when the boy indicates that he wishes to learn to speak Latin correctly. The Scholar says, "We beg you, O Master, to teach us to speak Latin correctly, for we are ignorant, and we speak badly." The Master asks, "What do you wish to talk about?" The Scholar replies, "We do not care what we talk about, as long as our speech is correct, and useful, and not foolish or base." (183) Because of the emphasis upon oral Latin in the liturgy and in view of the monastic practice of having Latin read at meals, it is not strange that the boy would feel the necessity for precision in speech. A sidelight on the Master's means of discipline and the boys' motivation for learning is indicated when the Master asks, "Are you willing to be flogged while learning?" The boy answers, "We would rather be flogged that we may learn, than remain ignorant, but we know that you are kindly, and that you will not lay strokes upon us, unless we oblige you to do so." (183) This last sounds like a teacher's model answer!

Even though the last part of the work must be assigned to Aelfric Bata and in general seems to place more emphasis upon the teacher, the picture of the daily life of the boys in the monastery must have been very close to that of Aelfric's time. The Master asks a boy what he has done that day. The boy answers, "I have done many things. This night, when I heard the call, I rose from my bed, and went out to the church, and sang nocturns with the brethren; then we sang of all the saints, and the matin song of praise; after that prime, and the seven psalms, with litanies, and the first mass, then terce, and we performed the mass of the day, after that we sang sext; next we ate and drank, and had our sleep, and rose up again, and sang nones, and now we are here before you, prepared to hear what you say to us." (193-194) Again from the last section one learns about the diet of the boys. They were allowed to eat meat because they were still young. In addition, they had vegetables and eggs, fish and cheese, butter and beans, and other "clean things." They drank water and beer, if it was available, but no wine. They slept in a dormitory. If they did not hear the rising bell, they were sharply roused by the master's rod. Also, in the last part, one notes a trace of wry humor. When a boy is asked if he had been flogged that day, he replies that he had not, for he behaved with caution. The Master then asks about his companions. The reply is, "Why do you ask me about that? I dare not reveal our secrets to you. Each one knows whether he has been flogged, or not." (194)

In the English preface to his *Grammar*, Aelfric expresses his belief that every man who has a valuable skill is obligated to invest it in other men, "lest God's money lie idle and he be called an unprofitable servant."[61] He hopes that his little book will provide the beginning of learning for the boys "until they come to greater scholarship." The three small textbooks must certainly have substantiated his hopes more effectively than any other pedagogical device then available to school-boys.

During his lifetime, Aelfric had seen the beginning of the great intellectual and spiritual revival in England which he points up dramatically when he says, "Before Archbishop Dunstan and Bishop Aethelwold reestablished monastic schools, no English priest was able to compose or understand a letter in Latin."[62] While he was still working quietly on the second volume of his *Homilies* in Cernel in 994, the Danes besieged London and plundered the east coast of England; in 1006 he was at Eynsham writing the life of Ethelwold when the Danish army was burning the towns and ravaging the countryside not far from his monastery. So Aelfric also witnessed not simply the end of the period of political stability and peace, but, more tragically, the destruction of much that had been accomplished during the brief era of the monastic restoration. It is not surprising, then, that one finds no mention of Aelfric's pupils or successors in the field of scholarship or education. Yet, by rare good fortune, Aelfric's books, and so his teaching, survived, as he was confident they would. In the prefaces of three of his works and at the end of two others he makes an earnest entreaty to anyone who may transcribe the book to correct it carefully by comparing it with the original to prevent errors that would contribute to false doctrine.[63] His confidence in the enduring power of the truth is expressed at the end of his treatise *On the Old and New Testaments* where he says, "Now maist thou well understand that the worke speaketh more than the naked sword, which profits not. Yet is there good worke ever in good words; as when a man teacheth and edifieth another in the faith of true doctrine."[64] Even during the terrible years immediately preceding and following the Conquest, the good words of Aelfric's books were being copied and read.[65]

A remarkably large number of these manuscript copies made during the tenth and eleventh centuries have survived to the present day.[66] The texts that have been edited from them have supplied Aelfric's modern disciples material for study in several fields. Scholars interested in his masterly handling of English prose, in his effective methods for presenting Christian doctrine in the *Homilies,* in his colorful recasting of Church history in the *Lives of the Saints,* in his unusual translation-adaptation of long passages from the Bible, and in his innovative system for teaching Latin to young boys still find Aelfric a gentle, thorough, and wise schoolmaster.

VII

Notker III
(ca. 950 - 1022)

Notker, the most learned of teachers—and the most gentle.[1]

EKKEHARD IV of the Benedictine abbey of St. Gall wrote an epitaph to commemorate four teachers from his monastery, all remarkably learned men, who were buried in the same grave.[2] They had all died of the plague which was brought back from Italy by the army of the German emperor, Henry II, in 1022.[3] One of the teachers was Notker III, whom the same poet, his pupil, calls "apertus," open, frank, and "doctrinae fomes," a tinder-box of learning. Apostrophising him, Ekkehard says,

> Notker, amor Christi, sacra libans corpore casto
> Symphona virgineis gaudia lude choris.[4]

The epitaph was a fitting requiem for the four masters, and for the whole school of St. Gall, because the death of Notker marked the end of the effectiveness of the school which had been one of the most active and influential in Europe.[5] From the galaxy of good teachers who had made the abbey famous for more than a century,[6] Notker shines forth as the most brilliant star.[7]

In order to distinguish him from Notker I (840-912), a noted poet, musician, and teacher, nicknamed "Balbulus," the "Stammerer," and from Notker II (d. 975), a noted physician and artist, known as "Piperis granum," the "Peppercorn," because of his hot temper, Notker III was often called "Labeo," on account of a prominent lower lip. Although no representation of him has been preserved, there is a verse description in which the broad lip is mentioned as his distinguishing feature, but the poet says that from this lip dripped honey.[8]

Notker III came of a noble family of Thurgau which had sent many of its members to the monastery of St. Gall where they gained the reputation of good scholars. Born about 950,[9] he also went there as a young child to be educated by the monks. In the absence of a biography, one must conclude from the abbey chronicles that he went under the auspices of his uncle, Abbot Ekkehard I, the poet, and he may have studied at some time under his cousin, Ekkehard II.[10] There is no record of his studies, but the educational pattern of the school is well known. In a letter to Salomo III, bishop of Constance,[11] who had been his pupil, Notker Balbulus outlines the course of instruction he gave the boys about the year 890. Beginning with the alphabet and the Psalter, he went on to teach them dialectic, then grammar and rhetoric, and finally the sciences of the quadrivium. A fuller account of the later educational system at St. Gall in Notker Labeo's time comes from a poem written by Walther of Speyer, in which he outlines his own education at the cathedral school in Speyer.[12] Written in 983 when Walther was only eighteen, it forms a long prelude to a poem on the life of St. Christopher, and was dedicated to his teacher, Balderich, bishop of Speyer, who had been trained by Gerald, the schoolmaster in St. Gall. Balderich's own school, founded about 970, was closely modelled upon the St. Gall school. After a thorough training in the Psalter and the offices of the Church, the boys read many Latin authors as part of their training in grammar. Walther mentions the Latin Homer, Virgil, Martianus Capella, Horace, Persius, Juvenal, Boethius, Statius, Terence, and Lucan.[13] The boys then turned to the other arts, studying rhetoric with the texts of Cicero, dialectic with Boethius' translation of Porphyry, then arithmetic, music, geometry, and astronomy through the texts of Boethius and Martianus Capella.[14] Some such course of study must have been provided at St. Gall for Notker.

Since Notker was a youth of keen intelligence, from a family with a long tradition for learning, apparently he needed nothing more than the usual training in the school of St. Gall, along with the opportunities for self-education afforded by the resources of the abbey library, to make him one of the finest scholars of his generation. When his own formal education came to an end, Notker continued in the abbey as a teacher and then as head of the school under Abbot Burckhard II. Of his teaching, some interesting information has been furnished by his pupil Ekkehard IV. Under the title *Benedictiones super lectores per circulum anni,*[15] Ekkehard assembled some fifty Latin poems most of which he had written as exercises in rhetoric when he was a student under Notker. Their origin is indicated by a series of marginal notations in Ekkehard's own hand, such as *Dictamen debitum magistro* and *Dictamen debitum diei magistro Notkero.* These metrical compositions, for which the teacher set the themes, mostly from the liturgical calendar and the lives of the saints, were found, after Notker's death, preserved in a chest in his cell,[16] and Ekkehard kept them to serve as models for his own students. Three of them are rather unusual in that they are concerned with "the confounding of the arts by the Church and the saints."[17] In them the poet points out how in the past the great mysteries of religion were often revealed without regard to the rules of grammar, rhetoric, and dialectic. Included with these school exercises is a poem addressed to Notker the schoolmaster,[18] and written to celebrate the holiday traditionally granted the students on the day after Epiphany,[19] but giving some interesting information about the master and his teaching. According to Ekkehard, as the Wise Men brought three gifts, so the festival brings three special favors to the boys: torches to prolong the festival into darkness, the luxury of a bath, and wine to celebrate their freedom.[20] The teacher is exhorted to participate in the holiday[21] and to let dialectic, rhetoric, and grammar sleep. In fact, begs the student, let all Parnassus sleep. Specifically do not resolve the lines of Persius, let the flute of Virgil be mute, let the mad Lucan put down the standards of

Pharsalus, let Statius fast, let the thorny verses of Horace be considered of no worth, let Ovid return into exile, and let Juvenal be bored with inactivity.[22] These references to subjects and authors give an impression of the substance of the studies taught in the trivium for the younger boys. That Notker also taught the older boys the sciences of the quadrivium is suggested when Ekkehard says, in the same poem, that on the holiday the students of the quadrivium play with the pupils of the trivium.[23] Notker's concern with the sciences is also indicated by an interpolation of his in his German translation of Boethius when he speaks about a celestial globe recently made in the monastery.[24] Further, his translation-commentary of the first two books of Martianus Capella suggest that he may well have taught all seven arts.[25]

On the same holiday, according to Ekkehard, the boys play all kinds of games, throwing stones, racing, and wrestling.[26] The poet asks that all disciplinary measures be suspended, that there be no reprimands, no whippings. The suggestion is made that the monitors should be silent and close their eyes to any peccadillos.[27] Finally, Notker himself is again exhorted to delight in the Elysian Fields.[28]

In his educational methods Notker, like Aelfric, was an innovator in making use of the vernacular at a time when only the youngest children were permitted to speak anything but Latin in school.[29] Ekkehard, in another poem in his collection, gives notice of some of the translations made for the first time from Latin into German by Notker.[30] In Ekkehard's manuscript, a gloss over the notice says that Notker translated these books "because of his affection for his pupils."[31] Notker himself, in a letter to his superior, Bishop Hugo II of Sitten,[32] explains that although he has renounced the study of the liberal arts except as they are instruments for the understanding of the Scriptures, he has set himself the unusual task of translating into German some of the standard authorities on the arts. Then, while he was translating the two treatises of Boethius, the *De consolatione Philosophiae* and the *De Trinitate*, he was asked to make a German metrical version of the *Bucolics* of Virgil, the *Andria* of Terence, and the *Disticha Catonis*. A further request came to translate the *De Nuptiis Mercurii et Philologiae* of Martianus Capella, Boethius' Latin version of the *Categoriae* and *De Interpretatione* of Aristotle, and an anonymous *Principia arithmeticae*. When this was finished, he devoted himself to translating the Psalter and the *Moralia* of St. Gregory. These German works won for Notker the title 'Teutonicus.'[33]

In his letter to Bishop Hugo, Notker explains that he knows the bishop will be shocked at this novel method of teaching, but he feels confident that gradually the works will become acceptable to him and he will come to see that for reading and understanding those books that are read with difficulty and comprehended imperfectly in a foreign language, the mother tongue will be very helpful.[34] Notker's translations were intended strictly for instructional use. His method was a complete departure from the usual method of studying the Latin texts. It had been customary for the teacher to supply Latin synonyms or definitions of individual difficult words in the text under consideration, and the early medieval manuscripts of the works of Boethius, for instance, reveal a text furnished generously with interlinear and marginal glosses in Latin. But in contrast to this, Notker presented the material in a form designed to give the student a consecutive interpretation of the thought of the author. He would present a sentence of the Latin text, then a literal German translation; in cases of particular difficulty he would give a paraphrase, often followed by a German explanation, sometimes derived from Latin glosses or commentaries. Occasionally he would introduce a paragraph as a summary at the end of a section of text. In this way the student would be in possession of the complete Latin text, the complete German text, and necessary explanatory material.

Of all these translations by Notker those that had the greatest impact upon education in later centuries in Germany were the first two books of Martianus Capella and Boethius' *De consolatione Philosophiae*, which he must have prepared for his advanced students. That he was able to render into clear, idiomatic German and then to explicate these two difficult texts, is, perhaps, the greatest proof of his instructional ability. First of all, it goes without saying that he himself understood the works thoroughly and knew the commentaries on them. In the form in which his translations have come down to us, they give the impression of representing the spoken words of the schoolmaster. For example, in introducing the first book of Martianus Capella, Notker cites the ninth-century commentary of Remigius of Auxerre,[35] which he uses extensively in his explanations. He had divided Martianus' first book into fifty-six short sections and provided for each a Latin heading to indicate the subject to be considered. After stating the title of the first section, he then proceeds to give the first Latin sentence, followed by the German version, supplemented by any explanation that would make the sense clearer, sometimes giving an appropriate reference to other classical works with which the student would be familiar. Presumably, before the master passed on to the next section, the students would have an opportunity to ask questions. The length of each section was conditioned by the relative simplicity or difficulty of the material. In this slow, thorough way, the students would have worked their way through the complicated allegorical setting of the encyclopedia of the seven liberal arts as presented by Martianus Capella[36] and through the philosophy of Boethius.[37]

Notker's achievement in his pedagogical practice of making translation-adaptations has merited praise,[38] but he has received more recognition for his consequent contribution to the German language.[39] In his letter to Bishop Hugo, Notker remarks that all German words, with the exception of the articles, must be written with accents, acute or circumflex.[40] He is very careful, too, to demand exactness in the pronunciation of consonants. One of his modern critics says, "He used and probably devised a most elaborate and phonetically exact system of orthography for German."[41] Although his subject matter was entirely expository and would seem to afford limited scope for literary niceties, yet his German prose has been hailed for its literary style[42] which has won for him the distinction of being "the father of German prose."[43]

Of the eleven translations of Latin texts into German which Notker himself listed in his letter, only five have survived. The lost works are Boethius' *De Trinitate,* the *Disticha Catonis,* Virgil's *Bucolica,* Terence's *Andria,* the *Arithmetica,* and the *Moralia* of St. Gregory. His most popular translation, apart from the Lord's Prayer, the Creed, and the Canticles, was the Psalter with annotations from the commentary of St. Augustine,[44] which was widely used and frequently copied in later times. Notker's own works, for none of which he would have claimed originality, were all based upon standard works and were intended as introductory texts for the instruction of his students in the liberal arts. In the field of rhetoric he wrote a short treatise that in his letter to Hugo he calls *Nova rhetorica.* A work consisting of fifty-nine topics relative to the material of rhetoric, its divisions and definitions of terms has long been considered Notker's.[45] It is almost entirely in Latin, with only an occasional German explanation, but it has three quotations from German poems to illustrate figures of speech.[46] On dialectic Notker wrote two short treatises on the most fundamental concepts of the art, the *De partibus logicae* and *De syllogismis,*[47] both in Latin but fully explained in German. On astronomy, he wrote a Latin *Computus,*[48] based on Bede's standard work of the same title, in which he furnishes the minimum essentials for determining the feasts of the liturgical year. On music he wrote four very short tracts on theory, the first known work on music in German, the *De musica,*[49] in which he explains the monochord, the tetrachords, the eight notes and the eight keys, and the measurement of organ pipes.

In addition to his work as schoolmaster and translator, Notker also served as librarian for the outstanding collection of books that had been assembled by a long series of scholars in the monastery library.[50] This responsibility would have demanded the entire time of a lesser man, for he had to concern himself with such matters as securing the expensive parchment,[51] and supervising the copying of the manuscripts in the scriptorium, and with the more difficult task of correcting faulty texts. Ekkehard testifies to his own assignment from Notker to erase certain scribal errors in a manuscript of Orosius and to restore the correct text by reference to two good copies.[52] It is known that Ekkehard himself copied the text of his own poetry, the *Liber benedictionum*,[53] and also wrote interlinear comments on the poems. Incidentally he pointed out two lines of corrected text which he says were written by Notker himself.[54]

This incomparable scholar, *impar eruditor*,[55] has been characterized as a gentle, kindly man.[56] True humility must also have been one of his most outstanding qualities, for in all of his varied writing, except for an occasional reference to the lakes and mountains, or a German proverb, so very little can be found to give any hint of the man that one must almost conclude that he deliberately sought anonymity.[57] By good fortune, in a poem by Ekkehard[58] a poignant account of his death succeeds in giving the essential flavor of his life. Stricken by the plague, he had just, that very day, finished his German translation of the *Moralia* of St. Gregory. Appropriately it was the evening of the feast of St. Peter for whom he had had a lifelong devotion. In the chapel of St. Peter he tearfully besought the brothers to sing the office of compline to insure a happy death for him. He made his confession, naming what he considered his greatest sin and one that continued to trouble his dreams, namely that once when a young man, while wearing his monk's habit, he had killed a wolf. He then asked that the poor be brought into his presence and given a meal. His last wish was that he be buried just as he was, in his habit, for he was unwilling that anyone should discover the great iron chain which he, in imitation of his patron, St. Gallus, had worn around his waist all during his life. The *Necrologium St. Galli* registers Notker's death under June 27, 1022, as: "Obitus Notkeri doctissimi atque benignissimi magistri."[59] A kind of epitaph, which may have been written by Ekkehard IV, occurs at the end of Notker's translation of the Athanasian Creed in an Einsiedeln manuscript:

Notker Teutonicus domino finitur amicus,
Gaudeat ille locis paradysiacis.[60]

Notker's most illustrious pupil and his successor as head of the
school was the poet, Ekkehard IV,[61] for whom he seems to have
cherished special affection.[62] His poems, gathered together under
the title *Liber benedictionum,* are chiefly concerned with the
liturgical calendar and the life of the monks of St. Gall. They
provide proof of the effectiveness of Notker's teaching, for
Ekkehard must be considered one of the most knowledgeable
scholars of his time. Besides his thorough acquaintance with the
Church Fathers, he knew and quoted the Latin poets from Ennius
to Juvenal,[63] and was familiar with Livy and Sallust. He did not
share his teacher's love for German, "a barbaric tongue," which
he seemed to think unsuited for scholarship.[64] His claim to fame
rests upon his prose history of the abbey during the tenth century.
This *Casus sancti Galli* is a continuation of the chronicle written by
Radpert, recording the history from the founding to the year 883.
While Ekkehard's work cannot be considered reliable history, it is
eminently successful in painting a picture of life in the abbey, in
depicting the outstanding members of the community, and in
describing the impact of outside forces upon the remote monastery. There one finds such stories as the account of the raid on the
abbey by the Hungarians in 925, the burning of the cloister in 937,
the attack by the Saracens in 954, and the tale of the remarkable
trio of friends, Notker Balbulus, Radpert, and Tuotilo.[65]

Another one of Notker's pupils, Batherus, who was forced by
his poverty to join the ranks of the wandering scholars, spent
several years in Spain and finally settled in a monastery on the
Moselle. There he wrote a biography of St. Fridolin and dedicated
it to his old teacher whom he characterizes as, "doctrina sophie
famosissimo meritorumque sanctitate beatissimo."[66]

Ekkehard pays the final tribute in his conclusion to the poetic
account of the death of Notker and the three other teachers when
he declares that God gave only to St. Gall and to St. Othmar, the
first abbot, schools capable of raising such men.[67]

7. *Notger of Liège kneeling before Christ offering his book. Cover of Notger's Evangeliary*

VIII

The Masters of the Diocese of Liège

Notger of Liège
(ca. 950-1008)

A very gentle teacher to the unlearned, a strong support to the old and weak, and a most zealous instructor of the young.[1]

GOZECHIN OF MAINZ, a former student at Liège, writing about 1050, describes to his own student, Walcher, the glory that had distinguished Liège a generation earlier: "That very flower of three-fold Gaul, that second Athens, flourished nobly in the study of the liberal arts and was exceptionally strong in the practices of divine religion." In fact, he adds, Liège had no reason to envy the Academy of Plato in the field of the arts nor any cause to envy the Rome of Leo IX in religion.[2] Recognition for the beginning of a great new era for Church and school in Liège must go to Bishop Everaclus, but the firm establishment and maintenance of this great intellectual and spiritual center, perhaps the foremost in the empire,[3] is due to Notger, bishop of Liège from 972 to 1008. That his great contribution to his city was recognized by his countrymen in his own time is attested by the tribute of one historian: "Liège, to Christ you owe Notger, to Notger you owe all else."[4]

Little is known of Notger's background,[5] except that he was of Swabian origin and probably of a noble family and may have been in some way related to the three talented Notkers of the abbey of St. Gall.[6] A young man of great ability and extraordinary zeal for learning, he may have received his early education from Bruno at Cologne.[7] At any rate, he acquired a thorough training in both the secular arts and in theology, though apparently he never received the habit of a monk. Very early he attracted the attention of the emperor, Otto I, and called to the imperial chancellery, he began a career of diplomatic service that lasted through three generations of the imperial family.

He was named bishop of Liège by Otto I and was consecrated at Bonn in 972 by the archbishop of Cologne. As a foreigner to his new episcopal see in Lotharingia, Notger found himself confronted with a very hostile situation both within his Church and with the feudal lords of the region. Only a man of the strongest resolution, inexhaustible energy, and firmest conviction could have restored order and discipline to his diocese as well as effecting a general working agreement with the secular powers as promptly as he did. Almost immediately he embarked upon a long-range program of building, including a cathedral, six churches, abbeys, enlargement of the city walls, other fortifications where needed, and bridges over the Meuse. The fine new city that took shape under his planning earned for Notger the distinction of being considered the "second founder" of Liège,[8] and he was called the *Pater patriae*.[9] At the same time, in his dual position as prince of the Church and counselor to the emperor, he was called upon to perform innumerable diplomatic missions. His official duties necessitated frequent sojourns at the court in Aachen and four journeys to Italy, once to assist at the coronation of Otto II by Pope Gregory V, and at another time to remain there with the emperor for five difficult years. It was his sad responsibility to accompany the body of the young emperor, Otto III, back from Italy and to preach at his funeral in 1002. In the following years of political turmoil, always loyal to the German emperors, he was successful in negotiating a treaty of peace between Henry II and the French king, Robert.

During his long career as churchman and diplomat which brought him into relationship with most of the political and ecclesiastical leaders of his generation, Notger also had opportunities to become acquainted with many of the outstanding scholars of Europe. Among these, he counted as his friends such diverse personalities as his old teacher, Bruno of Cologne, Bernward, the artist-teacher of Hildesheim, Adalbert of Prague, the poetic idealist who finally found peace in missionary work in the north, and Gerbert of Aurillac, the intellectual giant of the time.[10] Notger himself had a great talent for teaching and certainly one of his greatest contributions to the culture of his century was his promotion of education in the diocese of Liège. Inheriting the tradition for learning of the cathedral school, initiated by Everaclus, Notger took every means possible to encourage scholarship through the establishment and maintenance of libraries and schools. It is recorded that through his efforts the diocese had six lower schools in addition to the great cathedral school. This latter was divided into an interior school for the clerics and an exterior school for lay students.

Notger had such a love for teaching and such an intense interest in the education of the young men of his diocese that in spite of his many demanding duties, whenever possible he participated in the instruction of both clerics and lay pupils. One chronicler reports, "At the same time that he gave himself the joyful privilege of reading and studying the pages of Scripture with the clerics, he also instructed the pupils of the exterior school in subjects appropriate to their age and condition."[11] Though he had two natural assets of a stern teacher, the eyes of a lynx and the sharpness of a serpent, he always showed himself a very gentle teacher to the unlearned and a most zealous instructor of the young. He is credited with teaching the lay pupils in the vernacular and the clerics in Latin, "thus furnishing milk for the weak and solid food for the strong."[12]

For the interior school, that seminary for the clergy, Notger directed his efforts toward recruiting able students. To this end he did not restrict the school to freeborn pupils, but also took some children of servile origin. He also took boys from other dioceses if they were entrusted to him by their parents or their bishop.[13] He had the keenest interest in keeping in contact with these boys and watching their progress. Even on his numerous journeys he took the most promising of his young students with him, when under the direction of a chaplain they continued their studies, observing the same rigorous discipline as in the cloister. They carried along with them a supply of books and other classroom necessities. "And so it happened that those whom he took ignorant and illiterate often returned more learned than the masters whom they left."[14] In this way Notger prepared men for all types of service in the ecclesiastical hierarchy in that "nursery of clerics," as the cathedral school has been called.[15]

How very insistent he was to keep educated men in his schools is illustrated by the case of one of his students, Hucbald,[16] While he was quite young, Hucbald fled from the strict discipline of Liège and went to France where he attached himself to the canons of St. Geneviève. Before long he was teaching at the school and enjoying the respect and admiration of a great many students. For some time this escaped the attention of Notger, but when he became aware of the situation, by virtue of his episcopal authority, he ordered Hucbald to return to his diocese. Hucbald's departure from Paris was marked by many tearful farewells from his many friends, and he left many permanent influences of his teaching there. Some time later, when Notger was summoned to Paris by Henry II, the canons of St. Geneviève besieged him with humble supplications to permit them to have their old teacher, Hucbald, for at least three months of every year. The bishop gladly acceded to their wishes and by this generous act made Hucbald more eager to fulfill his obligations at home. Hucbald remained teaching at Liège until after Notger's death when he went to Prague to teach and eventually returned to Liège laden with honors.

Notger's talent as an administrator was demonstrated by his choice of excellent men to direct his various schools and to serve as masters. It is recorded, for example, that he invited Leo, a distinguished Greek bishop, a political exile from Calabria, to teach, and he remained in Liège for many years.[17] Notger selected Wazo, who had received his education at Lobbes, to direct the cathedral school at Liège and eventually Wazo served as bishop there. Anselm, in his chronicle of the bishops of Liège, says that Wazo "shone forth like Lucifer among the lesser stars."[18] In his analysis of the essential qualities of this brilliant master he says that such perfect harmony and singleness of purpose existed between Notger and Wazo that the two acted as one. Like his bishop, the schoolmaster was animated by the greatest enthusiasm for teaching. Both education in the liberal arts and moral training occupied his attention, but he valued pupils of high ethical standards above those who were merely proficient in letters. Of the many boys from other countries who sought admission to the school, he welcomed only those who demonstrated a serious interest in study. Anselm says that under the guidance of Wazo the school of Liège might be likened to a great tree full of fragrant flowers to which bees came from all directions to gather nectar, then to fly away to fill their hives with the honey they had gathered.[19]

Another very fortunate appointment that Notger made for the schools of his diocese was that of Heriger, a former student at Liège, then schoolmaster at the abbey of Lobbes, to the post of abbot of that monastery.[20] Like Notger, his long-time friend, Heriger loved to watch the progress of his pupils and continued to teach along with his new duties. In addition he collaborated with his bishop in a number of literary and expositional works. Because he thus proved such an important factor in carrying out Notger's educational program, his achievements merit him a separate section in this study.

From the diocese of Liège, that "fostering mother of scholarship" as the poet Adelmann of Chartres calls it,[21] a number of outstanding churchmen who counted themselves students of Notger went out to assume high positions in other churches—

Gunther, archbishop of Salzburg, Nothard and Eriliren, bishops of Cambrai, Haimo, bishop of Verdun,, Hezelo, bishop of Toul, Adalbold, bishop of Utrecht, and Durand, bishop of Liège.[22] Among those men who once studied under his guidance at Liège and then continued in the field of scholarship, several made outstanding contributions to education; for example, Hucbald who, as we have seen, taught at Paris, then at Liège, and later at Prague, and Egbert of Liège,[23] who during his years of teaching at his old school showed himself a most gifted and dedicated schoolmaster. His *Fecunda navis*[24] is based upon the principle that children learn not by fear of punishment, but by studying suitable and interesting material presented by a wise and sympathetic teacher.[25] Three more outstanding pupils of Notger gave their services to teaching in Germany, France, and the Low Countries—Gozechin, who wrote so enthusiastically in praise of Liège, studied further at Fulda and taught at Mainz; Adelmann, who later studied under Fulbert, taught at Chartres and wrote a famous poem on the scholars of his day; Franco who in his old school at Liège taught the sciences and wrote a number of treatises, especially on geometry.[26]

As a rich legacy to his Church and his country, Notger left the schools and churches he had built, while for the cultural advance of the age he left the innumerable scholars and teachers he had trained. Of his personal possessions, a single cherished relic is now preserved in his cathedral city, his magnificent Evangeliary.[27] This beautiful book was undoubtedly copied and decorated in his school during his episcopacy. The front cover has a remarkable ivory panel on which is represented in high relief the figure of Christ, seated, with a closed book in his left hand, holding up his right hand in blessing. The four corners of the panel are filled with the symbols of the Evangelists, each with his Gospel. In the foreground, at the foot of Christ, is Bishop Notger, kneeling before his episcopal throne, holding up his Evangeliary as an offering.[28] Around the outside of the panel is an inscription, probably composed by Notger himself, which reads:

En ego Notgerus peccati pondere pressus
Ad te flecto genu qui terres omnia nutu.

Heriger of Lobbes
(ca. 925-1007)

Among the learned, he was considered the most learned.[29]

DURING THE EPISCOPACY of Notger, the abbey of Lobbes, which had
been governed directly by the bishops of Liège from 889 until 959
when Everaclus gave it a separate abbot, became a notable
intellectual center in the diocese.[30] Chiefly responsible for the
physical rehabilitation of the abbey, the new and enlarged
buildings, the artistic enrichment of the church, and its protection
by adequate fortifications was its energetic and scholarly abbot,
Folcuin. In his *Chronicle* of the abbey from its beginnings up to his
own time, he indicates his interest in the development of the
schools and names three outstanding masters, including Ratherius,
of the generation before his time.[31] Yet, while acknowledging the
importance of Folcuin,[32] all agree that the reputation for scholarship which the abbey enjoyed was due largely to the schoolmaster,
Heriger, of whom one of his contemporaries said, "inter sapientes
habebatur sapientissimus."

In the absence of a contemporary biography, we must rely upon
the rather brief account in the supplement to the *Gesta abbatum
Lobiensium*[33] for facts concerning Heriger's life. Neither the date
nor the place of his birth is recorded. He may have come as a child
to be educated at the cathedral school of Liège, and he may even
have taught there. By 955 he was a Benedictine monk at Lobbes,
serving as *scholasticus* of the monastic school where he taught for
many years. He was a close and life-long friend of Bishop Notger

by whom he was commissioned to undertake several important historical works. The bishop also entrusted some of the diocesan affairs to him, and in 989 he took him to Rome on official business.[34]

In 990 Folcuin, abbot of Lobbes, died. The monks then wrote a most impressive letter to Notger, bishop of Liège, and to Rothard, bishop of Cambrai, their spiritual and temporal heads, asking to have Heriger made their abbot.[35] They first set forth the qualifications they considered important for the person who would have authority over their material and spiritual welfare, and ended with the stipulation that the future abbot should desire to be loved rather than feared.[36] They then declared that they had been able to discover no one better qualified in every respect than their old schoolmaster, Heriger. "For many years he has lived among us as a brother, bestowing great benefits upon us and fulfilling the role of teacher and counsellor most earnestly. We wish you to know that in his nomination we are unaminous. In common with us, you have the certainty that he knows how to teach well, that is, he knows whence he may draw from his storehouse both the new and the old." The request of the monks was honored and Heriger was consecrated abbot on the feast of St. Thomas in 990.

As abbot, Heriger fulfilled the Benedictine ideal outlined by the monks. He performed his administrative duties faithfully, also adding to the monastery buildings and making improvements for the adornment of the abbey. His chief concern, however, was the intellectual and spiritual enrichment of the monks, which was furthered by his teachings and his writings. As for teaching, Heriger was well endowed by nature and fully equipped by education.[37] Furthermore, he had under his jurisdiction the largest library in the Low Countries at that time. An early collection of books seems to have been increased by Folcuin who had a catalogue of the manuscripts made,[38] and no doubt Heriger also was responsible for adding volumes. Since Heriger had not studied outside of his diocese, there must have been available to him manuscripts of many of the classical authors, the Church Fathers, lives of the saints, works on liturgy and canon law, and textbooks on the seven liberal arts. From his writings it would appear that he taught the quadrivium[39] as well as the trivium.

The most convincing testimony to Heriger's ability as a schoolmaster comes from the scholars who were trained under him. Four stand out as distinguished for their contributions to scholarship and education. Olbert, abbot of Gembloux, who was from childhood a pupil at Lobbes where "he drank in something of the flavor of the seven arts, and could never satisfy his burning thirst for learning,"[40] was sent by Heriger for further study to Paris, Troyes, and Chartres, and became an eminent authority on canon law. A friend and fellow-student with Olbert at Lobbes, Wazo,[41] who was chosen director of the cathedral school at Liège and later was made bishop there, also became a noted canonist. Hugo,[42] abbot of Lobbes, and Theoderic,[43] reformer and abbot of the old house of St. Hubert, were known as excellent scholars and teachers. The most celebrated of the former pupils of Heriger were two illustrious churchmen: Burchard, bishop of Worms, and Adalbold, bishop of Utrecht.[44]

Heriger has the distinction of being the first historiographer of Belgium.[45] His *History of the Bishops of Liège,*[46] written at the request and with the cooperation of Notger, a chronicle of the diocese of Liège up to the death of St. Remaclus in 667, is a compilation of a vast amount of material from diverse sources. Written in a creditable style, it contains a great many literary references from the ancients as well as from the Fathers and the lives of the saints. Sometime after Heriger's death it was found and completed by Anselm, a canon of the cathedral of Liège.[47] Heriger's other historical writings, also inspired by Notger and sometimes attributed to him, fall into the category of hagiography. They are the biographies of several local saints: Remaclus,[48] Usmarus,[49] Landoaldus,[50] and Hadolinus.[51] All of these were intended for the instruction and edification of the monks and clergy.

More directly related to Heriger's teaching of the arts are two works in the field of mathematics. One is a treatise on the use of the abacus,[52] which was erroneously thought to be a commentary on Gerbert. The other is in the form of a letter in answer to seven questions of his student, Hugh, on the troubled matter of computing the date of Easter in view of the discrepancies between the computus of Dionysius and the calculations of Bede.[53] Another work on the question of the number of Sundays in Advent, written in the form of a dialogue between Heriger and Adalbold, bishop of Utrecht,[54] has been lost. No works to show his skill in music have been preserved, but he is credited with the composition of two antiphons in honor of his patron, St. Thomas the Apostle, and a hymn in honor of the Virgin.[55] In the field of theology Heriger undertook to support the orthodox view concerning the Eucharist against the heretical position of Ratramnus, by making a collection from the Fathers of the texts relating to the subject.[56]

Heriger's activities in writing were brought to an end apparently by the onset of blindness.[57] After seventeen years of fruitful service as abbot of Lobbes, he died in 1007 and was entombed near the altar of St. Thomas in the chapel of St. Benedict, which he had had constructed in the first days of his abbacy.[58]

IX

St. Bruno
Archbishop of Cologne
(925-965)

Christ, true Wisdom of the everlasting Father, gave him splendid gifts of such great knowledge that among learned men no one was ever more learned.[1]

ACCORDING TO LEGEND,[2] Poppo, bishop of Würzburg, once had a vision in which he was led to a high mountain where he saw a great city with beautiful buildings. Then, approaching a lofty tower, he climbed its steep ascent and upon its great summit was vouchsafed a vision of Christ seated with all his saints. There Bruno, archbishop of Cologne, was being accused by the Supreme Judge for his vain pursuit of philosophy. But St. Paul became his advocate and he was restored to his throne. It was fitting that St. Paul should vindicate Bruno, this dedicated man of God, who, though thrust into positions of power, had no other ambition than to spend his life learning and teaching in devout service to the Church. In performing these duties, we are told, "He shone out among all men of his time as the moon shines out among the lesser lights."[3]

Bruno was the single person in Germany in his generation who was sufficiently motivated and powerful enough to influence the restoration of learning throughout the empire. Born of the noblest Saxon stock, he was the youngest son of King Henry the Fowler and St. Mathilda, and brother of Otto I, the first German emperor. He was early appointed to strategic positions of authority in Church and state when he became successively abbot of Lorsch and Corvey, archbishop of Cologne, first chancellor of the

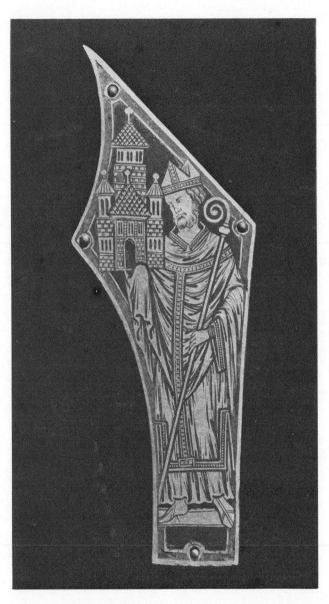

8. St. Bruno with the church of St. Pantaleon, Cologne. Copper gilt plaque with enamel by Nicholaus of Verdun

empire, duke of Lotharingia, and for a short period, when Otto
was in Italy, regent of the empire. If Otto, the soldier-statesman,
modelled his actions upon Charlemagne in gaining and unifying a
great empire, Bruno, the churchman and scholar, followed the
example of King Alfred in devoting his efforts to the arts of peace
by his promotion of a cultural and religious revival.

A biography of Bruno was written within two years after his
death, at the suggestion of Folkmar, archbishop of Cologne, by
Ruotger, a cleric at the cathedral, a man who had had a long
association with Bruno and the greatest admiration for him.[4]
According to his biographer, Bruno received as a heritage from
his mother a deep dedication to religion and from his father the
conviction that he was born for service to the state.[5] At the age of
four he was sent to Balderich, bishop of Utrecht, to be trained in
the liberal arts at the cathedral school which had gained a
reputation for excellence a generation earlier under the poet-
bishop, Radbod.[6] There the young boy, eager to learn and
scholarly by nature, received his first training in the services of the
Church in which he found great joy. In the school he soon
mastered Latin grammar and began reading the literature of the
ancients. He found the poetry of Prudentius especially congenial
since it combined Christian doctrine and ethic with elegance of
language and poetry—"the purest nectar."[7] He also read widely
in classical literature of both the Greeks and the Romans. Such
was his zeal for learning that he never permitted himself to be
distracted by idleness, levity, or the vain talk of his fellow-
students. His gentle nature could be roused to anger only by the
sight of someone mistreating or defacing a book. During nine
peaceful years he acquired the foundation of such distinguished
erudition in all branches of the arts and such wisdom and prudence
in public affairs that he was said to have surpassed all of his
contemporaries and even equalled the ancients.[8]

In 936, Bruno's brother, Otto, became king. Three years later
he summoned the young scholar to court at Aachen where he
planned to develop a Palatine school similar to the one Char-

lemagne had established. Though appointed chancellor and serving as his brother's advisor, Bruno first undertook the broadening of his own education. His biographer says that even amid the distractions of court life, he kept a strict regimen of study. Rising early, he guarded the morning hours for his books; after dinner, when others relaxed, he withdrew to his room to read or meditate. He studied the works of historians, orators, poets, and philosophers, investigating everything pertaining to the arts and philosophy. He even read the tragedies and comedies of the ancients, not (according to the biographer) to be moved by the subject matter, but to study the literary style.[9] During this time Bruno's official duties as advisor to Otto required him to leave Aachen and to travel frequently to other parts of the kingdom. On these occasions his school became peripatetic as he carried his library with him, protecting it "as if it were the ark of the Lord."[10] The library included both sacred and profane works, the former the object of his study and the latter the means to understanding them.[11] Even on the actual journeys he improved the hour by engaging in beneficial conversations or by meditation. Young as he was, he was considered to be a most able and prudent advisor to the king.[12] In all of this secular activity, continuing as *Deo dicatus,* he stood out as a supreme example of wisdom, piety, and justice. [13]

Bruno's higher education was not entirely the result of self-teaching. Otto gathered at his court a number of teachers of some reputation, and in whatever sphere of knowledge each excelled, there he made himself a humble pupil.[14] Often he engaged in philosophical and theological disputations with the most learned of these doctors, both Latin and Greek, for he was a skilled orator.[15] The Greek teachers were particularly impressed by his ability.[16] Among the foreign scholars who were attracted to the court school was Israel, an Irish abbot of Trier, an illustrious teacher, particularly proficient in Greek. From Verona, upon the invitation of Otto, came the brilliant bishop, Ratherius, to assume the place of "first among the philosophers."[17] The international diplomat and scholar, Liutprand of Cremona, spent some time at the court, during which he went on a political mission to Constantinople, and wrote a brief account of the reign of Otto.[18] Through the resources of these and many more unnamed masters, as well as by his own teaching, Bruno made the palace school one of distinction, where he trained promising young men for positions of responsibility in Church and state. The same school made Germany the center of a widespread intellectual and cultural revival. His biographer gives Bruno credit for most of this when he says, "It was he who rewove the pattern of the seven liberal arts that had long been obliterated."[19]

Bruno is called the *fortis athleta Dei* and *propagator Christianae fidei*[20] in a biography of his mother, St. Mathilda, where his labors for the propagation of the faith are described chiefly as they are seen in his work in establishing, reforming, and directing monasteries. He must have received the monastic habit shortly after his return to Germany, for he was still very young when he was given the responsibility of being abbot of the abbey of Lorsch and later of Corvey, in both of which he restored the Benedictine Rule. It is said[21] that even in the most difficult situations arising from the drastic changes necessarily made in the lives of the monks, this courageous champion of God never lost his native dove-like simplicity while at the same time he showed the shrewdness of the serpent as he led his reluctant flock back into an orderly community. Gentle with the humble, he was very severe with the stubborn and haughty; by kindly persuasion he won some, but he did not hesitate to use the disciplinary cane to rescue others from their errors. Ever a firm guardian of the truth, he first practiced what he taught others.

In 953 Bruno was elevated to the archiepiscopal throne of the see of Cologne,[22] a position of the highest importance at a time when internal rebellion and threats of violence from without were widespread. Bruno succeeded in establishing peace with his neighbors and gaining the loyalty of his own people to their king. He could then turn his attention to enlarging and adorning the beautiful old cathedral that had been started by Archbishop Hildebold over a century earlier. He also brought to it precious relics of St. Peter and other saints. In another section of the city he built the great church of St. Pantaleon with a monastery. Here in Cologne, too, he gave his attention to the cathedral school to which he invited distinguised scholars and teachers. The fine library which was left from the Carolingian bishops, together with the manuscripts he had collected on his journeys and those that were copied in his scriptorium, had a large part in making the school one of the best in Germany. As an administrator, Bruno was considered a model for all bishops.[23] The influence of his example was felt all over northern Europe, and it lasted long after his short life. The same year that Bruno assumed the duties of archbishop, he was made duke of Lotharingia, and thus became the secular as well as the ecclesiastical ruler of a very extensive territory. By governing justly, appointing worthy bishops, and by reforming old monasteries and building new ones, Bruno, the man of peace,[24] effected a harmonious union of Church and state.

When, in 961, Otto went to Italy to be crowned emperor, Bruno was given the guardianship, along with William, bishop of Mainz, of his young nephew, Otto, later to become Otto II.[25] Although the prince had other teachers, including Ekkehard II of St. Gall, Bruno can be given some credit for helping to inculcate in the boy a love for learning which he kept throughout his life. Another royal pupil who had the guidance of Bruno and the advantage of his learning for a short period was another nephew, Lothair, son of his sister, Gerberga, and Louis IV, king of France. Among Bruno's other pupils, Ruotger says the many great men who rose to high positions in the Church constitute a testimonial to his life, better than fine monuments.[26] Everaclus, whom Bruno named bishop of Liège, Gerard whom he chose as bishop of Toul, and Wikfrid, bishop of Verdun, were three of his most illustrious students who as teachers continued to follow his example. His cousin and dear friend, Theoderic, bishop of Metz, was his devoted disciple at the court school in Cologne where "in that gymnasium of the holy church of Cologne" he had been long trained in the liberal disciplines and admirably proven.[27]

Bruno's life came to a close when he was on an official mission at Rheims. Ruotger speaks feelingly of the reactions of Bruno's people as they visited his tomb in his beloved church of St. Pantaleon, praying for him and asking for his prayers. They reminded one another of what their bishop had done for them, what he had taught them, how he had lived and how he died. "As they look back over his years, they feel confident that from him some great thing will come for them or for their children."[28]

Sigebert, the biographer of Bishop Theoderic of Metz, gives his judgment upon Bruno's impact on his generation, when he says, "Rightly would I declare the times of Otto fortunate since the government was formed by famous leaders and wise men, peace was restored to the churches, the integrity of religion was reborn. One might see proven that saying of the philosopher: fortunate is the state if the kings are wise or philosophers rule. For there were ruling over the people not hirelings, but famous shepherds. Among those who by their own merit must be compared to shining stars, that greatest magnitude ever famed and deserving of fame shone forth, Bruno, archduke and archbishop, like the blazing star of morning."[29]

9. St. Wolfgang with the Cathedral of Regensburg

X

St. Wolfgang of Regensburg
(ca. 930-994)

An extraordinary talent for teaching
was given to him by God.[1]

As in the myths of the Greek heroes, the future brilliance of St. Wolfgang was portended before his birth when it seemed to his mother that she was carrying a star.[2] Born of noble Swabian parents,[3] the child was baptized "Wolfgang," a name that he translated "Lucambulus" or "Walking Wolf."[4] His biographer, Othlo, a learned monk of St. Emmeram in Regensburg (Ratisbon), wrote an account of his life not long after his death.[5] This, with another, shorter account written by Arnold, also a monk of St. Emmeram,[6] constitutes the chief source of information concerning Wolfgang. Othlo says that when the talented child, who also had the gift of poetry, was seven years old, his parents entrusted him to a priest to be instructed in his letters. In but a few years, with his great eagerness for learning, "thirsting for the divine waters of life," he not only mastered the substance of the Scriptures, but was seeking out the very marrow of their mystical meaning. No longer content with private instruction, he asked to be sent to the monastery of Reichenau where the school enjoyed great prestige. Welcomed there because of his unusual intelligence, he soon won the respect of all.

At Reichenau, Wolfgang formed a firm friendship with one of his fellow students, which had a lasting influence upon his life. Henry, a young man related to the royal family, persuaded

Wolfgang to go to Würzburg to attend the cathedral school, where the bishop, Poppo, had brought a noted Italian scholar, Stephen of Novara, to·serve as teacher. After the young men enrolled in the school, all went well for a time, but one day the master was reading the difficult allegory of Martianus Capella's *Marriage of Mercury and Philology* and was unable to explain some irregularity of the meter. As they had done before, the other students went to Wolfgang and asked him to explain the meter, and obligingly Wolfgang answered their question, then went further, revealing to them the significance of the whole difficult passage. When the master discovered this, moved to wrath, he prohibited Wolfgang from attendance at his lectures. Thereafter Wolfgang was obliged to study without a teacher, but he made astonishing progress. Only the urgent request of his friend, Henry, however, kept him from leaving to take up the life of a solitary.

In 956 Henry was made archbishop of Trier. Reluctantly Wolfgang went with him, but he resisted all offers of ecclesiastical honors and benefits with the excuse that he was unworthy. At last he consented to serve as schoolmaster, reasoning that by using his God-given talent for teaching he would emulate the faithful steward of Scripture. His only condition was that, unlike the majority of masters, he would receive no remuneration; he would work simply to enrich others. The young men whom he endeavored to teach he trained not simply in the liberal disciplines, but also in moral philosophy. The instruction he gave was tempered to the ability and experience of the individual pupils. For the more able he expounded the most difficult and abstruse matters; then, turning to the illiterate and simple youths, "like a nurse" he supplied them with the most elementary knowledge.[7] Moreover, the poor and forlorn who came under his tutelage, he refreshed with both material and spiritual sustenance. His own daily routine furnished a splendid example of holy living for them. He had the opportunity to further his self-education in the resources of the fine library of the monastery of St. Maximin where he became a close friend of the scholarly abbot, Ramwold, who was himself a distinguished teacher.

Archbishop Henry persisted in his efforts to promote his friend to a position of greater responsibility in Church or monastery, and finally persuaded him to serve as dean of the canons of the cathedral school. Immediately Wolfgang brought the young men into regular community living in accord with the monastic reforms being introduced into Germany at that time, and he himself observed the austerities of a religious life. After the early death of Henry, Wolfgang wished to leave Trier and retire to his native Swabia, but Bruno, archbishop of Cologne, invited him to his see and offered him high positions, even that of bishop, if he would remain in Cologne. Although he would accept no office, thus demonstrating his singular dedication to his own ideal, he stayed at Cologne for some time. Finally, with reluctance, Bruno permitted Wolfgang to return to Swabia.

If Wolfgang had been besieged by offers of honors and positions of power in Cologne, at his home among his well-intentioned relatives, he was like Ulysses among the Sirens.[8] Beset by the pleadings of his friends and by promises of a larger legacy from his family, he argued his case with the support of the Gospels and the Fathers. Finally, having asked his family to divide his inheritance among them, he withdrew to the remote abbey of St. Mary at Einsiedeln in the forest near the Bodensee in 968. He chose this secluded spot because the community observed a strict rule under the English abbot, Gregory, a man of the greatest dedication.[9] Shortly after Wolfgang received the Benedictine habit, he was made teacher, giving his pupils training in the classical authors and in the seven liberal disciplines, along with spiritual instruction. His success soon attracted students from far-distant monasteries as it also caught the attention of the prelates of the Church.

This was the kind of life Wolfgang would have chosen to continue, but as a result of a visit of the learned Bishop Ulric of Augsburg to Einsiedeln, Wolfgang became an *agontheta Dei,* a warrior for the Lord.[10] Ulric had recently returned from Pannonia where he had helped secure the defeat of an invading Hungarian horde, and he was seeking missionaries to evangelize those fierce people. Influenced by his eloquent plea and by the expressed wish of the emperor, Otto I, but moved to action by a vision in which St. Othmar revealed his future to him, Wolfgang was ordained a priest by Ulric and soon set forth on his mission to the Magyars. He was engaged in this new endeavor for only a year when his superior, Bishop Piligrim of Passau, recalled him to undertake another assignment. Although Wolfgang persisted in his reluctance to accept administrative positions, finally, under pressure from his bishop, the clergy, and the people, yielding to the will of the emperor, he was consecrated bishop of Regensburg.[11] Thereafter, for twenty-two years, he, bishop in the habit of a monk, labored courageously and forcefully for his diocese. One of his first concerns, and one that proved a difficult task to accomplish, was the regularization of the great monastery of St. Emmeram which had earlier merited a good reputation for scholarship. For this purpose he sent to the abbey of St. Maximin in Trier for his old friend, Ramwold, and with his assistance, succeeded in restoring the strict Benedictine Rule. Turning his attention to the library, Ramwold repaired old neglected manuscripts, including the famed Codex Aureus,[12] the gold-lettered Gospel book of Charles the Bald, restored the usefulness of the fine collection of books, and added many more volumes. Through the efforts of abbot and bishop, St. Emmeram with its good school, library, and scriptorium became the intellectual center of Bavaria.

In Regensburg, Wolfgang reformed two convents and the monastery of St. Paul, while in the surrounding areas he instituted the restoration of five more. His next work was to establish canon law in his diocese. Besides the time he had to spend on these and other episcopal duties, he was obliged to participate in numerous other functions as prince of the Church. A staunch supporter of the emperor, Otto II, he attended numerous synods and diets and often took extended journeys on diplomatic missions. When he was in the city, he found time to supervise the studies of the young monks at St. Emmeram. After the death of Ramwold, he designated the course of study for the various students, and he frequently examined the written work of those who showed themselves especially competent in the liberal arts. He even held out the promise of special privileges to stimulate the earnest students, and he reproved the laggards.[13] For the most part his own teaching had to be limited to his preaching as he visited the various churches of his large diocese. In this art he was most successful, for, in spite of a speech defect,[14] he was remarkably eloquent and drew great crowds of listeners whom he stirred to deep emotion.[15] None of this kept Wolfgang from living a simple life, observing his private devotions and personal austerities as strictly as any monk. In fact, his great personal purity and integrity, coupled with his kindness and compassion, gave rise to accounts of miracles performed through his virtues, even during his lifetime.[16]

As evidence of his intellectual talents, his biographer describes a demonstration of Wolfgang's dialectical skill as he, at the behest of Otto, debated with a certain heretic on the dual nature of Christ.[17] Among his spiritual gifts he had the power of prophecy which was evidenced in his prediction of the future lives of the children of Duke Henry of Bavaria.[18] Even after Wolfgang's death, he is said to have appeared to the young Henry in a vision[19] and foretold his reign as Henry II.

Of the many students who felt the inspiration of learning under the direction of this talented and saintly teacher, the records name the four children of Duke Henry: Bruno, bishop of Augsburg; Brigida, who became a nun; Gisela, wife of King Stephen I of Hungary; and Henry II, emperor of Germany,[20] who gained a great reputation for wisdom and achieved such distinction in his Christian vocation that even in his lifetime he was known as St. Henry. Two prominent churchmen, Tagino,[21] archbishop of Magdeburg, and Poppo,[22] son of Margrave Liutpold, later archbishop of Trier, are said to have received instruction from Wolfgang.

A legendary account[23] which developed in the fourteenth century from an incident in the life of Wolfgang when he withdrew from Regensburg for a short time to a monastery at

Mondsee in the Alps is responsible for many of the artistic representations of the saint. He is often depicted with an axe in his right hand and a crozier in his left.[24] According to the legend, once when Wolfgang became discouraged by the political intrigues in his own diocese, he retired into the dense forest not far from Salzburg, determined to spend the rest of his life as a hermit. He selected the spot where he should build his cell by throwing an axe, asking God to direct its fall. There, near a lake which was later named for him, he devoted himself to prayer and meditation. Meanwhile his people sought for him in vain until a hunter happened upon his refuge. Thereupon the bishop, though reluctantly, returned to Regensburg. So great was the virtue of this holy man that, legend says, when he left, his very cell wished to follow him. According to the official interpretation in the *Acta Sanctorum,* the story demonstrates the fact that God was unwilling to have his saint hide his light, but rather wished to have him place it where it might shine forth for the whole Church.[25]

XI

St. Bernward of Hildesheim
(ca. 960-1022)

Like a bright jewel shedding radiance upon his country's heritage.[1]

WHEN THE BEAUTIFUL and ambitious empress, Theophanou, widow of Otto II, sought a German-born tutor to teach her seven-year-old son, the powerful archbishop of Mainz, Willigis, recommended a young Saxon priest, Bernward, who was already distinguished for his knowledge of the liberal arts, his experience in diplomatic and ecclesiastical affairs, his religious vocation, and his personal charm.[2] Some years later, when Bernward, elected bishop of Hildesheim, was leaving the court, Otto III, in affectionate remembrance of the devotion of his teacher, presented him with a fragment of the True Cross. As an reliquary for this precious gift, Bernward himself fashioned a beautiful wooden processional cross, inlaid with gold and set with pearls and gems, and had a chapel built to house it.[3] This holy relic became the focus of Bernward's plans for the spiritual enrichment of his see as he devoted many years to building in its honor a monastery and a great church dedicated to St. Michael the Archangel.

The names of Bernward's parents have not been recorded, nor has the year of his birth, but he is known to have come from a noble Saxon family from the vicinity of Hildesheim, and he was born about 960.[4] Very likely he had some academic training from a local priest before he was presented by his uncle, Bishop Folkmar of Utrecht, to be given a liberal education and moral training[5] at the cathedral school of Hildesheim. At the time, the school, under

puer Bernwardus claro nr̄e g̅e̅n̅i̅s̅ sanguine
ex filia athelberonis palatini comitis· tradi
tur· domno Osdago nr̄o epō· a suo auunculo re
liguoso diacono folcmaro· post quoq̄ traiec
tensi antistiti· & amborum diligentia meę
paruitati· qui primicerius scolę puerorum
preeram· literis imbuendus· moribus etiam
instituendus deputatur: Quem omni deuo
tione susceptum· intellectus illius capacitatē
primo diuinę paginę leuiori lacte temptan
dam estimaui· Mox itaq̄ ut de sc̄o daniele
legitur: inueni in illo decuplum in omni intel
ligentia sup coetuos eius· Mirum namq̄; in mo
dum tenera ętas celesti irradiata lumine· sub

10. *Minature of St. Bernward in manuscript of Thangmar's* Vita

the control of Bishop Othwin, a man who had been educated at Reichenau and who had great enthusiasm for collecting books,[6] had a reputation for good monastic discipline as well as a tradition for both the liberal and the mechanical arts. The bishop was fortunate to have as head of his school and also as librarian a Saxon scholar, Thangmar. This wise and understanding teacher, who later wrote Bernward's biography, received the boy with a kindly welcome, then almost immediately, in order to test his ability, set him to reading and memorizing some passages from the Bible. Thangmar reveals that, like Daniel, ten times more intelligent than the other boys, and already revealing a divine illumination, Bernward was not satisfied to read the passages, but with the help of the more gifted of the older pupils, tried to discover the hidden meaning of the words. Apparently because he was new and perhaps younger than the others, Bernward was seated in a far corner of the classroom, but "like a most prudent bee" he listened intently to the master's lectures on various books, then secretly imparted his knowledge to some of the other boys who had not grasped the subject. When Thangmar became aware of the keenness of mind and the seriousness of purpose of this young pupil, with the support of the bishop, he took special care to stimulate his natural interest in learning.

Since Thangmar also served as the bishop's secretary, he had frequently to travel about on episcopal affairs, and took the young boy with him to give him the benefit of private lessons and a more profound study than was possible in a large class. He was strongly impressed by Bernward's manifold excellences, far beyond his age. "We often spent the whole day studying as we rode, at one time reading no less widely than if we were in the classroom, at another time we diverted outselves composing poetry; then, turning to exercises in prose, we sometimes discussed a question in its simple context, often we labored over syllogistic propositions. Sometimes, he also, though in a modest manner, put to me very acute questions taken from the very depths of philosophy. His searching mind was so attuned to mine that scarcely an hour, not even one devoted to refreshment, charged him with idleness."[7]

The academic training Bernward received at the school included the seven liberal arts, theology and philosophy, and perhaps something of medicine[8] and canon law. Thangmar himself was so completely oriented to the academic studies, that he tends to underestimate the other arts that Bernward was acquiring, when he says, "Though his mind was afire with the most lively enthusiasm for all liberal disciplines, nevertheless he also made a study of the lighter arts which are called 'mechanical.'"[9] Then he gives an account of Bernward's proficiency in calligraphy as demonstrated in the copying and illuminating of manuscripts, in the art of the goldsmith and the jeweler, and in painting, as well as in architectural decoration. Because of these skills and because he proved most efficient and tactful in all community efforts, he was highly esteemed by bishop and clerics alike. Thangmar remained his loyal friend and served as his confessor throughout his life.

At the time when it might be expected that Bernward would himself begin to teach at Hildesheim, at the wish of his maternal grandfather, a Palatine count who was his guardian, he went to the larger episcopal diocese of Mainz for further training in theology under Archbishop Willigis. Enjoying great prestige and exerting a powerful influence over ecclesiastical decisions in Germany, Willigis was a vigorous administrator who maintained an efficient school, carried on an extensive program of building, and even supervised the workshops where the manual arts were being carried on. Bernward undoubtedly spent time in the school studying theology, but he profited more particularly by the skills he perfected in the mechanical arts and by examining the art treasures which the bishop had assembled during his trips to Italy. After he had been ordained deacon and priest,[10] his career was interrupted for several years which he spent in the country caring for his aged grandfather, but he made several journeys to Utrecht to visit his uncle, Bishop Folkmar, where he had a good opportunity to observe the very active reform movement in the monasteries of Lotharingia. While he was there, he refused the offer of the post of abbot of Deventer[11] and remained with his guardian until his death in 987.

Bernward then went to Nymwegen to become one of the royal chaplains at the court of Theophanou, the Greek widow of Otto II, who was acting as regent for her seven-year-old son.[12] Shortly thereafter, on the recommendation of Willigis, or because the empress had time to assess his talents and personal qualifications, she appointed Bernward tutor to the young Otto. Under his guidance, the precocious young king made great progress in his studies and gained experience in the ways of court life. Although others flattered the boy, and his mother, eager to keep his affection, indulged him and agreed to anything he desired, Bernward alone managed with great tact to hold him to some kind of discipline and at the same time to keep his respect and maintain a cordial relationship. After his mother's death, Otto remained for several more years under the tutelage of Bernward for whom he cherished a singular affection.

During his six years at court, Bernward made a number of official journeys to other cities where the German emperors had established royal residences. From the art treasures in these palaces, particularly from the beautiful works left by Charlemagne at Aachen, and from the remarkable collection that Theophanou had assembled at Nymwegen, he became acquainted with some of the finest art work of Europe and even of the East.

On January fifteenth of the year 993, Archbishop Willigis consecrated Bernward bishop of Hildesheim,[13] and for the next thirty years, this devoted servant of God, always loyal to the emperors, took action to protect his people against aggression from without, strove to strengthen and reform the ecclesiastical structure of the diocese, undertook a program of building to ennoble his episcopal city, and sponsored the creation of works of art to beautify his churches, so that Hildesheim became "the art capital of northern Europe."[14] Although he spent more time in his diocese than his contemporary bishops, since the Church in Germany was so closely bound to the state, he was obliged to attend numerous synods and participate in imperial conferences. His noteworthy journeys outside of Germany included a visit to

Rome in the year 1001, when his former pupil, Otto III, honored him by coming out to meet him at the city gates and then entertained him in his palace.[15] In the six weeks he spent in Rome, after his official business was transacted, Bernward made a thorough tour of the city to study the great works of ancient art and architecture that still remained. On another occasion, after finishing a political and military mission in Lotharingia, he made a pilgrimage to the shrine of St. Denis in Paris and of St. Martin at Tours, at the same time studying ecclesiastical art in northern France.[16]

In spite of these activities, his biographer says that Bernward maintained for himself the discipline of a monk, and that although he was moderate in every other respect, he was immoderate in using the night hours for reading.[17] So great was his desire to learn that when he dined he always had some book read to him. At this time his teaching seems to have been centered in his work at the palace library. With Bishop Othwin's unusually fine collection of manuscripts as the center, Bernward gathered a splendid library of philosophical and theological writings.[18] Further, he founded scriptoria in the monastery and in other places.[19] Himself a fine calligrapher and illuminator,[20] he took great pains to instruct the students and to supervise the masters who were entrusted with copying and illuminating texts. Unfortunately a fire that swept through the cathedral in 1013[21] destroyed much of the library, so the activity of producing books must have been increased after that time to make up for the losses,[22] but of the many manuscripts that were copied and decorated in the cathedral scriptorium, only five are still extant as witnesses of Bernward's own skill and his proficiency as a teacher—a Bible, three Evangeliaries, and a Sacramentary, all carefully written and richly illuminated.[23] One of the Evangeliaries has a large painting of Bernward offering the very book at the altar to the Mother of God.[24] The colophon of the same manuscript, written in Bernward's own hand,[25] states that he had the book written for the church of St. Michael, and he threatens a curse upon anyone who may steal it.

While Bernward was honored as a bibliophile and a scholar, he won greater recognition for his work in the creative arts. A life-long student of art, as sculptor, painter, goldsmith, and architect, he was largely responsible for what has been called "the Ottonian renaissance."[26] Here, too, one important part of his work was that of teaching, and that may be considered under three aspects: his actual instruction as a master of apprentices, the pictorial representations of Christian doctrine on two of his major architectural works,[27] and the indoctrination of the worshippers into the glory of their religion by providing his church with the most precious and beautiful ritual objects. All of the arts in which Bernward was skilled himself were carried on in the cathedral workshops. Thangmar says that he regularly went to these, supervising and directing the work.[28] When he discovered boys of unusual talent, he took them with him on his various journeys, as Thangmar had taken him, teaching them and stimulating their imaginations by showing them fine examples of workmanship of every kind.[29]

As an architect, Bernward planned the great church of St. Michael upon which he lavished his personal fortune and for its adornment designed and had cast two unusual works of art. The first was a great column sheathed in bronze, inspired by the column of Trajan in Rome.[30] On a spiral band circling the column eight times, he made twenty-eight panels, each depicting a scene from the life of Christ from his baptism in the Jordan to his triumphal entry into Jerusalem on Palm Sunday. Executed in a simple, forceful style, with naturalistic figures, this was a kind of pictorial Bible to instruct the unlettered in the basic facts of the life of the Master. Bernward's second great architectural master-piece was a pair of bronze doors for the same church. Patterned upon the great doors of the church of St. Sabina in Rome, they presented the whole theme of Christian theology. On the left door, in eight scenes, the artist depicted the Creation and the Fall, while on the right, again in eight scenes, he portrayed the passion and death of Christ.[31] No doubt with these visual presentations the preacher could make cléarer to his unlettered people the great Christian mysteries from the creation and fall of man through sin to his redemption through Christ's atonement.

Finally, Bernward helped to make the Christian ritual a more awe-inspiring and beautiful experience for his people by designing and executing numerous ecclesiastical articles used in the liturgy. These range from his early work, the reliquary for a fragment of the True Cross in the form of a processional cross, which I have already described, to chalices of gold, patens of silver, crucifixes adorned with precious stones, censers, candlesticks and candelabra, and covers of service books magnificently resplendent with gems and gold and silver.[32] More effectively than words, the rich and beautiful objects must have taught the worshippers the priceless gift of their religion.

The key to the inspiration of Bernward's heart and the motivation of his work may be considered his great devotion to St. Michael the Archangel, the leader of the hosts of heaven against the power of Satan and his armies. The very number of churches in northern Europe besides Bernward's splendid edifice[33] attest the widespread belief that St. Michael was still bringing and would continue to furnish help for men's salvation.[34] As St. Michael overpowered the forces of evil and darkness, so Bernward enlisted his aid in fighting against the darkness of ignorance and in bringing the light of knowledge to his people. It is recorded that when Bernward's tomb was opened in 1194,[35] the year after his canonization, at his sides were found two candlesticks engraved with his name, on which were wrought curious designs. Fortunately they are still preserved in St. Magdalen's church in Hildesheim.[36] Composed of a combination of precious metals, their stems are like tree trunks covered with leaves and grapes; climbing up from the base are grotesque men and animals; nearer the top are angels and birds also advancing toward the light. The whole scene was intended to symbolize the light of salvation victorious over the powers of evil and darkness. It is not remarkable, then, that in the epitaph on his tomb in St. Michael's church, ascribed to Benno, bishop of Meissen, Bernward should be likened to "a bright jewel shedding radiance upon his country's heritage."[37]

11. *Gerbert. Detail from an ivory bowl used at the coronation of Otto III in 996*

XII

Gerbert, Pope Sylvester II
(ca. 945-1003)

The pupil's victory is the master's glory.[1]

"WHEN GOD wished to rekindle a great light in Gaul which was then covered with darkness, He put it into the minds of Duke Borrell and Archbishop Hatto to make a pilgrimage to Rome. With them they took the young Gerbert."[2] In this dramatic way the historian Richer introduces a significant episode in the early life of the greatest and most brilliant schoolmaster of the tenth century, Gerbert of Aurillac. Born near Auvergne in the province of Aquitaine, of humble parents, probably some time around 945, Gerbert received his earliest education at the neighboring monastery of St. Gerald at Aurillac,[3] one of the houses that Odo of Cluny had restored to the Rule of St. Benedict and where he served briefly as abbot. There the young Gerbert received spiritual training and sound instruction in Latin grammar and literature under two unusually fine and gifted men, the abbot Gerald and the teacher Raymond, later abbot. Richer gives no further information concerning Gerbert's years at Aurillac until 967 when the count of Barcelona, Borrell, came to visit the monastery. Abbot Gerald took the opportunity to ask if he might send one of his monks to Spain to be instructed in the sciences. So it was that Gerbert, chosen unanimously, went to Vich in Catalan Spain to study under the supervision of Bishop Hatto. For more than two years he studied the mathematical arts and acquired a remarkable knowledge of arithmetic, music, geometry, and astronomy.[4] He also made lasting friendships with three Spanish scholars, Guarin, abbot of Cuxa,[5] Lobet of Barcelona,[6] and Bonfill, later abbot of Gerona.[7] Then, when Borrell and Hatto, wishing to found a new archbishopric in Catalonia, went to Rome in 970, they took Gerbert with them. Gerbert's sojourn in Italy, as Richer points out, proved not only a turning point in the life of the young scholar, but it marked the start of the revitalization of scholarship in France.

Immediately upon his arrival at Rome, Gerbert became associated with the greatest personalities of Church and state of his time. Pope John XIII, impressed by his knowledge of mathematics, kept him in Rome where "music and astronomy were completely unknown."[8] By the pope, he was presented as one "remarkably learned in mathematics and prepared to teach it with vigor"[9] to the emperor, Otto I, who took him to his court in Ravenna, hoping to have him assist in the education of his son, Otto II. From that time on, Gerbert's meteoric career in the diplomatic world as advisor to emperors and "maker of kings,"[10] as well as in the ecclesiastical world, though often against great obstacles, from abbot of Bobbio, archbishop of Rheims, and archbishop of Ravenna, to bishop of Rome, as Pope Sylvester II, belongs to political and Church history. Our concern must be limited to Gerbert's activities in scholarship and teaching, where he achieved phenomenal success and great acclaim among his contemporaries.[11] The passage of time has not negated their estimate of his place in the history of scholarship, for Gerbert has been called "the first mind of his time, its greatest teacher, its most eager learner, and most universal scholar,"[12] and has even been named "among the great teachers of all time."[13]

While Gerbert was in Italy, although he enjoyed the favor of both pope and emperor and his future was assured, his chief ambition seems to have been to complete his own education by mastering dialectic. By a fortunate coincidence, the archdeacon of Rheims, Gerannus, who had the reputation of being an excellent logician, had been sent by Lothair, king of France, on a diplomatic mission to Otto. So it was arranged that Gerbert should study dialectic under Gerannus, and he was granted permission to travel to Rheims with the prelate and in return to teach him mathematics and music.[14] With his mastery of the last of the seven liberal arts, Gerbert's formal education came to an end, but with the inquiring mind and persevering application of the perennial student, he continued the process of self-education throughout his lifetime. For example, somehow he acquired a knowledge of medicine, for which he gained a wide reputation.[15] He himself regarded the broad field of philosophy as his chief end, as he testifies that he was tossed about much on land and sea while he was pursuing the discoveries of the philosophers.[16] While others speak of his learning in terms of light,[17] he seems to prefer the figure of thirsting after knowledge, which he considered the very sustenance of life.[18] Richer aptly expresses his endless zeal for study when he says, "Fervebat studiis"—there was a passion for learning within him.[19] To his friend, Abbot Ebrard of Tours, Gerbert wrote his simple formula for living, "Equally in leisure and in work we both teach what we know and learn what we do not know."[20]

At Rheims, during the time he was studying logic under Gerannus, Providence, says Richer, directed him to the attention of Archbishop Adalbero who was seeking a master for his cathedral school.[21] This enlightened scholar, a pupil of John of Gorze and himself a reformer, was responsible for the rehabilitation of the school which had had great prestige in the time of Archbishop Hincmar under the masters, Remigius of Auxerre and Hucbald of St. Amand. So Gerbert, ordained to the priesthood by Adalbero, entered upon a career of teaching and, with the exception of a year as abbot at Bobbio, experienced the happiest years (971-989) of his life. He brought the school to a high degree of excellence as students from every quarter flocked to his classes. One of the few schoolmasters of his time capable of teaching all seven disciplines, Gerbert found opportunities to put into execution his theories of education. Accordingly, he departed from tradition by introducing new methods of study, by restoring the classics to an important position in the curriculum, by inventing and using a number of practical teaching devices, and by training his students for positions of high responsibility in Church and state.

Gerbert always considered a good library an absolute necessity for teaching. At Rheims he fell heir to what remained of the fine collection of books that had been assembled largely through the efforts of Bishop Hincmar.[22] At this time, in a very reduced state, it consisted chiefly of theological and patristic writings, but also of some of the standard school texts. Immediately Gerbert instituted a search for the books he needed and he continued to press his hunt throughout his teaching years. One of his letters to the abbot of Tours bears witness to his method. "Just as a short time ago in Rome and in other parts of Italy, in Germany also, and in Lorraine, I used large sums of money to pay copyists and to acquire copies of authors, permit me to beg that this be done likewise in your locality."[23] To the same purpose he wrote to former students, to his friends in Spain, and to various abbots of monasteries in which he knew that manuscripts were preserved. Some of the books he requested are works of Cicero, Caesar's *Gallic Wars,* Victorinus' *De rhetorica,* Boethius' commentary on Aristotle's *Periermenias,* Boethius' *Astronomia,* Statius' *Achilleis,* Pliny, Eugraphus' commentary on Terence, and several books on arithmetic, geometry, and astronomy.[24]

From Richer, who had received his own education under Gerbert, comes information concerning the master's plan of study and methods of instruction. Apparently Gerbert as *scholasticus* received the older students after they had been trained in grammar on the works on Donatus, Priscian, and Martianus Capella, for he first introduced them to dialectic and then went on to rhetoric. Of the arts of the quadrivium, he first taught arithmetic, which he considered basic to the mathematical disciplines, then music, then geometry, and finally astronomy.

By beginning with dialectic, Gerbert reversed the ordinary

procedure, convinced, apparently, that the student must first learn to organize and analyze his thoughts before considering effective methods for expressing them. According to Richer,[25] in teaching dialectic, he began by reading and explaining Porphyry's *Isagoge* or *Introduction* in the Latin translation of Victorinus as his text, using the commentary of Boethius as supplementary material. This was followed by the study of Aristotle's *Categoriae* which he analyzed and explained. Then he elucidated the *Periermenias* or the *De Interpretatione*. This was culminated in a study of the *Topica*, the foundation of all proofs, from the translation of Cicero, with the help of Boethius' extensive commentary. In addition, he read and demonstrated in a practical way Boethius' works on dialectic: the four books *On the Topical Differences,* the two *On the Categorical Syllogisms,* the three *On the Hypothetical Syllogisms,* and the book *On Defintions,* and the *On Division.* Thus Gerbert seems to have been the first of the medieval teachers to have used all of the treatises of the *Logica vetus* of Aristotle in Boethius' translations and following Boethius' commentaries, many of which he was fortunate enough to possess.[26] Undoubtedly Richer mentions the very extensive course in dialectic because it was so unusual, and he adds that Gerbert made the material understandable by his very clear explanations. The same corpus of teaching material continued in use by Fulbert of Chartres, his pupil, and later by Berengar, Lanfranc, and Abelard. As an aid to teaching dialectic Gerbert devised a chart to show the various divisions into which material for logical consideration must be classified. It was a deliberate misrepresentation of this chart that gave occasion for what proved to be a very famous debate between Gerbert and Othric, a leading scholar of the German school of Magdeburg. This disputation, held at Ravenna, with the emperor, Otto II, as sponsor, demonstrated Gerbert's skill both in logic and in rhetoric as he demolished his opponent's arguments on a question of dialectical classification.[27] Gerbert's own interest in logic never left him, and in later life he wrote for the emperor, Otto III, a *Libellus de rationali et ratione uti,* a discussion of the question as to whether the use of reason can properly be predicated of a rational being.[28]

Gerbert was unorthodox and practical in his approach to rhetoric also. Richer says, "After a long study of these works (in dialectic), he wished to have his students pass on to the art of rhetoric, but he felt that it was not possible to advance to the art without a knowledge of the modes of diction which can be learned only from the poets. Therefore he used those poets with whom he felt the students should be familiar. He read and expounded the poets, Virgil, Statius, and Terence, as well as the satirists, Juvenal, Persius, and Horace, and the historical poet, Lucan. When his students had familiarized themselves with these authors and their stylistic methods, he introduced them to rhetoric."[29] Surely he must have treated the chief prose writers also, for Gerbert took great pains to acquire the works of Cicero, his favorite author and a great comfort in some of his bitter troubles.[30] Perhaps at his advice, his pupil Richer took Sallust for his model in writing history.[31] In the course of his writings, Gerbert mentions a great many other authors whom he must at least have called to the attention of his students. This method of teaching rhetoric was a departure from the usual practice of the monastic schools because of his attitude toward the classics. In most of the monasteries that had come under the influence of the Cluniac reform, the pagan poets were considered superfluous, if not dangerous influences. One recalls the story of Odo's dream of the perils of reading Virgil;[32] a successor of Odo at Cluny, Maieul, when librarian, took pains to excise from the books of ancient philosophy and other secular works the passages that dealt with love and other unsuitable subjects.[33] Gerbert's own knowledge of the classics made him suspect in the ecclesiastical world, as one sees when, in 995, the papal legate, Leo, for political reasons, opposed his elevation to the archbishopric of Rheims, but gave as his objection that "the disciples of Peter must not have as their teacher a Plato, a Virgil, a Terence, or any other of the herd of philosophers."[34]

We are not told what books Gerbert used to teach rhetoric, but surely they included works of Cicero, Cassiodorus, and probably Martianus Capella. In a letter to Rainard of Bobbio,[35] Gerbert asks to have several books copied for him, among them Victorinus' *De rhetorica* which may have been Victorinus' commentary on Cicero's *De inventione.* In a letter to Constantine,[36] he asks him to bring Cicerno's *De re publica,* the *In Verrem,* and as many of the orations as possible. Writing to the monks of Aurillac, he describes a teaching device which he invented to simplify the difficult art. He says, "I constructed a certain table of the rhetorical art arranged on twenty-six sheets of parchment fastened together in the shape of an oblong, made of two sheets by thirteen sheets—a work truly wonderful for the ignorant, and useful for the studious for comprehending the fleeting and very obscure materials of the rhetorician and for fixing them in the mind."[37] For their practical training, he turned his students at Rheims over to a special tutor who gave them practice in speaking and in disputation.[38] In this way their proficiency in grammar, dialectic, and rhetoric would be demonstrated. His goal was that they should learn to express their thoughts in an orderly and efficient way and that they should seem to speak without the assistance of the art. In this respect, of course, training in the cathedral school differed from that in a monastic school. Many of Gerbert's students were being prepared not for the contemplative life, but for active careers as effective administrators in the ecclesiastical hierarchy.[39]

Gerbert's long study of the arts of the trivium did not lead him into metaphysics, as one might have expected, but rather served to reinforce his conviction that they should be taught for their practical value. For him, "the art of arts" was neither dialectic nor theology, but "the guidance of souls."[40] Similarly, his knowledge of the sciences of the quadrivium, which might have directed him to theoretical speculation or to experimentation, challenged him to make understandable to his students the practical application of the principles of the mathematical disciplines, and to make tools to assist in the process.

While all agree on Gerbert's proficiency in science, the source of his knowledge has not been absolutely determined. As a young man he went to Spain with the stated purpose of learning mathematics and there he had competent masters, but it is not known if he had any direct contact with Arabic science through Moslem teachers, or if his acquaintance came indirectly through the Christian schools there.[41] At all events, he was familiar with the works of the Moslems, and in teaching mathematics at Rheims, he began, according to Richer, with arithmetic as basic to all the sciences. Normally arithmetic was treated as a theoretical subject dealing with the nature, properties, and relationships of numbers, as set forth by Cassiodorus and Martianus Capella. Of course, Gerbert had to concern himself with number theory, as one sees in a letter to a former student who had asked him to explain a passage in Boethius' *Arithmetic,*[42] which Gerbert may have used in class. In later years, presumably Gerbert had sent a manuscript of the same book to the emperor, Otto III, who was then studying the liberal disciplines, for Otto wrote asking him to explain it to him.[43]

One of the greatest deterrents to the advance of the science of arithmetic had always been the cumbersome Roman numerals. Although Gerbert cannot be credited with first introducing the Hindu-Arabic numerals into European lands north of Spain,[44] unquestionably he played a very great part in transmitting this clear and economical method of notation as he used it in his own teaching. The most conspicuous witness to his use of this notation is the abacus that Gerbert had constructed to teach arithmetic and geometry to his pupils. Richer describes it.[45] "He had an abacus, that is, a board that could be divided into compartments, made by a shield-maker. Its length was divided into twenty-seven parts, on which he arranged nine symbols representing all the numbers. He also had made out of horn one thousand counters inscribed with characters which, placed within the twenty-seven compartments of the abacus, provided for the multiplication or division of any number, dividing or multiplying these great numbers with such rapidity that one could comprehend the answer by sight more quickly than by explanation." To his class Gerbert would have demonstrated the manipulation of the abacus, showing them how to arrange the counters in each of the twenty-seven compartments, leaving a vacant space for the zero, which was not in use at that time.[46] In 980 Gerbert wrote to his former student, Constantine, then in Fleury, explaining the abacus and indicating its wide usefulness.[47] There is also a short treatise attributed to Gerbert explaining the abacus.[48] Gerbert did not invent the abacus, which had, indeed, been used by the Moslems, yet he is sometimes given credit for it,[49] and his name was so closely associated with it that people came to call one who used the abacus a "gerbertist."[50]

Since at the time geometry was chiefly used for the very practical purpose of surveying, it was appropriate that Richer should mention the abacus when discussing Gerbert's work in geometry. For teaching the principles of the science, he would have used the conventional texts, illustrating the various theorems with his own diagrams. That he did devise figures for teaching geometry is made clear from a letter of Adalbold of Liège, written when Gerbert was archbishop of Ravenna. Adalbold had asked him to send some geometrical figures in addition to those which he had already sent, along with a manuscript containing several treatises on surveying.[51] The introduction to Gerbert's own treatise *De geometria*[52] stresses the practical value of the discipline as he follows the Roman rather then the Greek authorities.[53] The work itself is an elementary text, treating the common geometrical figures, but it concentrates upon methods for measuring land, heights, depths, enclosures for cattle, etc. His advanced students went beyond these simple processes, for in the letter to Adalbold he gives an explanation of the difference between arithmetical and geometrical procedures for finding the area of a triangle. His talent lay not in innovations, but in making available to his students this very important area of technical knowledge.

Gerbert was also credited with using the astrolabe. A *Liber de astrolabio*, traditionally attributed to him but long rejected by modern scholars, has now been accepted as his work.[54] His immediate followers, at any rate, had unbounded faith in his skill in determining distances, for one of them says that he could easily measure spaces both on earth and in the sky merely by looking at them.[55]

Richer says that Gerbert made the art of music famous, though it had been largely unknown in Gaul before his time.[56] Here, again, Gerbert dealt with the practical side of the discipline, as he used the monochord to determine true pitch. "By arranging the various notes on the monochord, breaking up its consonants or symphonic unions into tones and half-tones, also into major thirds and quarter-tones, accurately separating the sounds into tones, he restored the perfect knowledge of music."[57] Unfortunately Richer does not explain further and only gives the assurance that Gerbert was reaffirming the principles established by Pythagoras. From other sources one learns that Gerbert used organs to teach practical music. In a letter to Bernard of Aurillac, he recommends his former pupil, Constantine, not only to teach rhetoric but also to give instructions in music and the playing of organs.[58] Apparently he knew how to construct an organ and had one constructed as a gift to his old monastery.[59] In several letters he mentions organs of his that were being kept in Italy.[60] Of course, one must assume that Gerbert also taught music theory. In two letters to Constantine[61] he undertakes to elucidate difficult passages in Boethius' *De musica,* which he may have used as a basic text.

What textbooks Gerbert used to teach astronomy is not known.[62] He speaks of having discovered Boethius' lost *De astronomia* at Bobbio,[63] and later asks to have it copied,[64] but this treatise is unknown to us. He quotes Martianus Capella's *Astronomia,*[65] a book which was commonly found among the compilations of astronomical texts. He followed Pliny and the information in Isidore of Seville's *Etymologiae,* as well as Hyginus, and Macrobius and Cassiodorus. Richer gives no information on this subject, but he was greatly impressed by his teacher's effectiveness in presenting this difficult discipline, and he fully described four astronomical models that Gerbert constructed for his classes. The first[66] was a solid celestial globe made of turned and polished wood covered with horsehide. On it he located the north and south poles at the intersections of the two circumferences at right angles, then with compasses he determined the arctic and antarctic circles, the two tropics, and the equator, all of which he painted red. Finally, he painted on it, also in colors, the constellations of the northern and southern hemispheres.[67] The globe, supported through the poles and fitted into a framework so that it could be revolved, was slanted on the circle of the horizon for the latitude of Rheims. By means of this sphere Gerbert could make clear the configuration of the heavens, the parallels, the ecliptic, and the location of the stars. By revolving it, he could demonstrate the rising and the setting of the various constellations. Thus he taught the stars.

His second teaching model[68] was a planetarium, the chief function of which was to make clear the revolutions of the planets. He first constructed an armillary sphere, on the inside of which he joined the two colures intersecting at the poles. Then he fashioned the five parallels, and divided each hemisphere from north to south into thirty parts. Across the parallels, he made an oblique circle, the ecliptic, the path of the zodiac. Within the circle, by a very ingenious mechanism, he suspended the orbits of the various planets. Undoubtedly he placed a model of the earth on the central axis which supported the sphere, for by this device he could demonstrate the paths of the seven planets, their heights, and their distance from one another in a geocentric universe.[69]

Having provided these two classroom models to teach the students the relation of the earth to the planetary system and the pattern of the heavens, Gerbert turned from the theoretical to the practical, by taking his students out of doors to observe the celestial phenomena at night. Richer says, "At night he turned his attention to the brilliant stars and had his students observe how they move in an oblique direction from their rising and their setting over the different parts of the world.[70] In order to assist his students to see and identify the various stars and constellations, he contrived a curious device which must be regarded as a precursor of the telescope. Richer describes it in some detail,[71] but Gerbert himself in a letter to Constantine who had requested information gives more explicit directions both for its construction and for its use.[72] He started with a solid wooden sphere upon which he had marked the two colures, divided into sixty parts, the north and south poles, and the five parallels. He then divided the sphere into two hemispheres by cutting it on the circumference from the north to the south poles. One hemisphere was then hollowed out and holes were bored at the intersections of the five parallels and at the poles. Into these openings six-inch viewing tubes were inserted. The hemisphere was held in place by an iron semicircle corresponding to the circumference and bored with similar holes. The end viewing tubes were then slanted toward the north. For its operation, Gerbert says, "When our polestar can be observed, place the hemisphere which we have described under the open sky in such a way that, [looking] through the tubes at the extremities, you may perceive the polestar itself by an unobstructed view. If you doubt that this is the polestar, station one tube in such a position that it does not move during the whole night and look toward that star which you believe to be the polestar. If it is the polestar, you will be able to see it through the whole of the night; if it is any other star, it will not be visible through the tube because it will have changed position. Therefore, having placed the hemisphere in the aforementioned manner so that it is immovable you will be able to determine the North Pole through the upper and lower first tube, the Arctic Circle through the second, the summer through the third, the equinoctial through the fourth, the winter through the fifth, the Antarctic [Circle] through the sixth. As for the south polestar, because it is under the land, no sky but earth appears to anyone trying to view it through the tubes."[73]

Richer emphasizes that the purpose of the instrument was to make real to the students the imaginary parallel circles.[74] The purpose of the viewing tubes, of course, was to afford a view of single stars unaffected by the light of others. Gerbert's other observing instrument, described too briefly by Richer,[75] was an armillary sphere, apparently having only the two colures, but none of the parallels. On the outside he represented the stars and constellations, attaching them to the framework by means of iron and copper wires. Through the center, for the axis, he placed a hollow viewing tube which represented the poles. Richer says that most remarkable thing about it was that even if a person knew nothing about the stars, if one constellation was identified for him, he could locate the others without the help of the teacher.[76]

These unusual accomplishments of Gerbert, particularly in the sciences, when he was master of the cathedral school of Rheims, are all the more remarkable because his term of service extended little over ten years. After his appointment as counselor and secretary to Archbishop Adalbero in 984, he had to devote most of his time to Church affairs. Further, the unequal record of Gerbert's teaching and his ingenious devices reveal little of the essential quality of the man or his attitude toward learning and teaching and his relationship to his students. In some measure this lack can be supplied from references in his own letters to his former instructors and those to his pupils. Perhaps only after he had experience in teaching did Gerbert realize fully how forturnate he had been in the monastery at Aurillac to have had Abbot Gerald to direct his training in Christian doctrine and Raymond to teach him grammar and literature. Not only his affection for his old abbot but his great reliance upon his advice are indicated in a letter Gerbert wrote from Rheims in 985 after he had been forced from his untenable position as abbot of Bobbio.[77] In it he says, "In such changeableness of things, of sorrow, fear, joy, desire, his son Gerbert particularly asks the opinion of his most trusted Father Gerald as to what course should be followed." At the same time, he wrote again to Gerald, "I do not know whether the Divinity has granted anything better to mortals than friends . . . Fortunate day, fortunate hour, in which we were permitted to know the man, the recollection of whose name has deflected all annoyances from us."[78] Other letters reveal notices of his gifts of vestments sent to him, and the promise of one of his organs.[79] In 987, at the death of Gerald, Gerbert wrote, "Bereft of my illustrious Father Gerald I do not seem to survive as a whole man."[80]

A number of letters to his old master, Raymond, show his continued love and gratitude to him. When Raymond was elevated to the abbacy of Aurillac, Gerbert wrote, "Not only do I rejoice at your honor, but Father Adalbero rejoices . . . all the more sincerely, the more you shine with the light of religion and learning."[81]

Upon his own election to the archbishopric of Rheims, Gerbert wrote to Raymond and the monks of Auillac, "Be with your son, reverend fathers, and render him aid by prayers poured out to God." He continues with one of the finest tributes ever given to any teacher, "The pupil's victory is the master's glory." Finally, he gives thanks to all of them, "but more especially to Father Raymond, whom, after God, I thank above all mortals for whatever knowledge I possess."[82]

At a difficult time in his life when Gerbert was caught in a political power struggle and immobilized so that he was unable even to help his friends, he wrote to his old monastery concerning his activities, saying, "Meanwhile, I offer to noble scholars the pleasing fruits of the liberal disciplines to feed upon."[83] That Gerbert's teaching was never simply the brilliant performance of a virtuoso can be judged from the evidence of a close personal relationship between master and pupil which lasted long after the students had left Rheims. Attention has already been called to several letters to Constantine, schoolmaster at Fleury and later abbot of Micy, in which Gerbert answers his former pupil's queries concerning problems of arithmetic and the abacus, music, and astronomy, and to one in which he recommends Constantine as a teacher of music.[84] Gerbert, too, asked a favor of his pupil when he urged him to bring some of the manuscripts of Cicero's works to Rheims.[85] He calls Constantine, "sweet solace of my labors,"[86] and says, "Only the compulsion of friendship reduces the nearly impossible to the possible."[87] With another pupil, Remi of Trier, later abbot of Mettlach, Gerbert continued on an easy, friendly relationship for many years. He addresses him as "sweetest brother," and he speaks in a series of four letters[88] about a sphere which he had undertaken to construct at Remi's request. In what one may interpret as a playful mood, Gerbert asks him to have a copy of Statius' *Achilleis* made for him in payment. When Remi sent an incomplete copy, not only because his exemplar was incomplete, but because the poem had never been finished, apparently unaware of this, Gerbert calls attention to the incomplete transcript, but promises to deliver the sphere, though it was a year's work. A third pupil and lifelong friend, Richer, a monk of St. Remi at Rheims, dedicated his *History of France* to his old master, and in his own unending pursuit of the liberal arts attests to the efficacy of Gerbert's inspiration.[89] In recording the ever-increasing number of students who came to hear Gerbert, he says, "The fame of such a great doctor was spread not only throughout parts of Gaul but also to the peoples of Germany; it even crossed the Alps and passed into Italy as far as the Tyrrhenian sea and the Adriatic."[90]

It is said that "at least thirteen of Gerbert's pupils became bishops or archbishops, and five or six more abbots of principal monasteries."[91] Through the influence of these carefully trained churchmen, learning was restored or reinvigorated in many monastic and cathedral schools in northern Europe. The most outstanding men among these administrators were Adalbero, bishop of Laon, Jean, bishop of Auxerre, Adalbold of Utrecht, Heribert of Cologne, and Fulbert, master of the famous school at Chartres and later bishop.

Among his pupils Gerbert could also name two monarchs, Robert the Pious of France and Otto III of Germany. When Gerbert was at Rheims, Hugh Capet chose to send his son, Robert, to the cathedral school to be educated in the liberal arts rather than to the monastic school of Fleury under Abbo.[92] The father chose wisely, for at Rheims Robert received an education suitable for a king. In contrast to his father who did not even speak Latin,[93] Robert had a good knowledge of theology and canon law which served him well on numerous occasions, and his knowledge of the arts and particularly his skill in music made him one of the best educated rulers of his age.[94]

The young emperor, Otto III, like his father and his grandfather, was keenly interested in learning and a great admirer of the brilliant intellect of Gerbert who had shown himself a faithful supporter of all three rulers, and was in a large measure responsible for winning the throne for Otto III. At a time when Gerbert's fortunes were at a low ebb as his claim to the archbishopric of Rheims was contested and he was in virtual exile, Otto wrote a charming and tactful letter inviting him to the court at Pavia. "Otto himself writes to Gerbert, most skilled of masters, and crowned in three branches of philosophy. We wish to attach to our person the excellence of your very loving self, so revered by all, and we seek to affiliate with ourself the perennial steadfastness of such a patron because the extent of your philosophical knowledge has always been for Our Simplicity an authority not to be scorned. . . . We humbly ask that the flame of your knowledge may sufficiently fan our spirit until, with God's aid, you cause the lively genius of the Greeks to shine forth."[95] So Gerbert undertook to complete Otto's education, particularly in philosophy,[96] and it proved to be a very happy experience for both. Gerbert remarks upon the unusual situation: "I do not know what more evidence of the divine there can be than that a man, Greek by birth, Roman by empire, as if by hereditary right seeks to recapture for himself the treasures of Greek and Roman wisdom."[97] Under Gerbert's tutelage, Otto, that "stupor mundi," pursued his purpose to appropriate his heritage of the Graeco-Roman culture and dreamed of reestablishing a universal Roman Empire. Apparently a truly sincere friendship existed between the elderly scholar and the young ruler, if one can take at face value Otto's salutation,

"Otto, most faithful of his pupils in steadfast perseverance, to Gerbert, master beloved above all others."[98] In 998 Otto elevated Gerbert to the archbishopric of Ravenna and in 999 to the Holy See, and Gerbert became Sylvester II to his Constantine.[99] Then there was for a short time hope that a great dream of the harmonious union of the universal Church and the empire might be realized. An Italian poet, Leo of Vercelli, wrote: "Rejoice, Pope, rejoice, Emperor, let the Church rejoice; may there be great joy in Rome, may the palace be jubilant. Under the power of the Emperor, the Pope is purifying the world. You twin beacons, shine upon the churches throughout the earth, drive away the darkness, so that one may be strong through the sword, the other be heard through the word."[100] Unhappily Otto never saw the fulfillment of his vision, for he died in 1002 at the age of twenty-one. Gerbert survived his distinguished pupil by only a year.

Gerbert, the great teacher and master of all human knowledge, became the subject of legend shortly after his death. In a satirical poem written in the eleventh century, Adalbero, bishop of Laon, represents King Robert as saying, "That famous master Neptanabus taught me a great many things."[101] Here Gerbert is designated by the name of the sorcerer king of Egypt, Nectanebus, who plays an important role in the legend of Alexander the Great. Because Gerbert's learning was more extensive and more advanced than that of most of his contemporaries, because he had spent some time in Spain acquiring knowledge of the sciences, and because he exhibited rare skill in contriving mechanical devices, he fired men's imagination and more marvels were attributed to him than to any other personage in the Middle Ages.[102] According to one "authority," William of Malmesbury,[103] writing in the twelfth century, Gerbert when a young man ran away from the dull monastery life at Fleury, where he had been brought up, and went to Spain in order to study astrology and related sciences under Saracen teachers. There he learned the arts of the quadrivium, but he also studied augury, necromancy, and other forms of magic. He tried desperately, but in vain, to acquire a certain book on magic from his master. Finally, with the help of the magician's daughter, he stole the book and fled. Pursued over land and sea, he was saved only by making a pact with the devil to serve him forever. By means of his illicit arts he uncovered treasures once buried by the ancients. His most spectacular success was discovering the incredible golden treasure trove of Octavian. Another feat that Gerbert performed through his knowledge of astrology was that of fashioning the head of a statue which could speak and answer questions like an oracle. Even Gerbert's actual achievements were distorted. It is said that he stole the abacus from the Moslems and then made up cunning methods for using it. A sundial which he made for a church at Magdeburg became a marvellous clock that performed in a mysterious way. His organs became more complicated; they were hydraulic engines which, when heated by steam, emitted harmonious sounds from their pipes.[104]

Far more remarkable than the fictitious magical feats and even than the actual mechanical instruments he constructed, the real legacy of the teaching of Gerbert was the spirit of humanism that motivated all of his activities relating to his work as a teacher and shows itself in his writings.

Gerbert, the Benedictine monk, educated in two monasteries, who served as abbot of Bobbio, archbishop of Rheims and of Ravenna, then as Pope Sylvester II, never questioned Christian doctrine and never considered himself other than a loyal son of the Church.[105] Yet his own self-education and the instruction that he gave his pupils went far beyond the bounds that, at the time, limited the training given in Christian schools, so that he can rightly be considered a humanist.[106]

In the first place, Gerbert's formal education was much more extensive than that usually given to a monk. In addition to grammar, he studied the Bible and the Fathers at Aurillac; in Spain he became acquainted with the works of science, including some of the results of Moslem learning; at Rheims he mastered dialectic and became a skillful orator. Stimulated by this learning, his thirst for knowledge drove him to collect manuscripts from every available source. These included chiefly the Roman poets, orators, and historians, works on rhetoric, Boethius' translation of the Greek works on dialectic, the encyclopedic writings of Martianus Capella, Isidore of Seville, Cassiodorus, and Macrobius, and everything possible on science. As Gerbert studied these texts throughout his life, he sought to reclaim, as far as he was able without a knowledge of Greek, the whole spiritual and intellectual heritage of the West. From his diverse experiences in the world and from his vast reading, Gerbert developed his own philosophy, which to him was the science of all things divine and human, a synthesis of the speculative and the practical, that would embrace all of the arts, ancient philosophy and literature, and Christian theology.[107]

Gerbert was essentially a teacher during all periods of his life, even when his administrative duties kept him from the classroom. His mind was stocked with a richer store of knowledge than any of the men of his time could claim, and his zeal for communicating what he had acquired to his students was nowhere surpassed. Possessing a keen, analytical mind, the master of a lucid style, in his rigorous instruction of the arts of the trivium he strove to teach his disciples how to order their ideas and to express them clearly and convincingly. In teaching the sciences he presented them also as practical tools for seeking out the truth. He regarded his students as his friends and took great satisfaction in following their academic progress long after they had left his school. No closet philosopher, he spoke freely about the joys of sharing the great treasures of learning with kindred minds, the true humanist ideal.

Gerbert showed little interest in seeking fame through writing books of his own. The few that he did write were in response to some immediate problem and are all expository.[108] It is in the large collection of his letters that one finds expressed his concern for a wide diversity of people and his interest in their problems. In the letters one sees that Gerbert was an admirer of the finest literary works of antiquity both for their beauty of style and for their expression of universal human values. Cicero, whose noble prose he emulated, was his favorite author. At a time of great stress, when the city of Rheims was besieged, he wrote to the abbot of Sens, who had sent him some manuscripts of Cicero; " . . . In my opinion, nothing in human affairs is preferable to a knowledge of the most distinguished men which assuredly is unfolded in the numerous volumes of their works. Continue as you have begun and offer the waters of Cicero to the one who thirsts. Into the midst of the cares that enveloped us after the betrayal of the city, Marcus Tullius so obtrudes himself that in the eyes of men we are considered happy, but, in our judgment, unhappy."[109] On occasion the Christian Gerbert's reflections on human life might easily be confused with the pagan Cicero's. Writing to his old teacher, Raymond, concerning his failure to maintain his place as abbot of Bobbio, he says, "For these cares philosophy alone has been found the only remedy. From the study of it, indeed, we have very often received many advantageous things; for instance, in these turbulent times, we have resisted the force of fortune violently raging not only against others, but also against us."[110] When he addresses Bishop Thietmar of Mainz, it might be Cicero speaking. "Let it be characteristic of our friendship to desire the same things and to be averse to the same things. Moreover, because, amid the burdensom anxieties of cares, philosophy alone can be a certain relief, may your industry supply whatever parts of it we have incomplete."[111] Cicero's disciplined mind, his elegant Latin, and his Stoic acceptance of life made a strong appeal to Gerbert, but in many ways Boethius was more spiritually akin to him.[112] Boethius' interest in all of the arts, his expository works on almost all of them, his great contribution in translating Aristotle's chief works on logic, as well as his ability to surmount his great personal misfortune, made a strong impression on Gerbert. This admiration was communicated to Otto III who took occasion to honor the memory of Boethius by erecting a monument to his memory, for which Gerbert composed an epigram. These verses have been lost, but a similar poem which was inscribed on the base of a portrait of Boethius has survived.[113] The achievements that Gerbert singles out for praise are the fact that he was "patriae lumen," the light of his fatherland, and that he shed light on learning, and was not inferior to the genius of the Greeks. From these two authors, Cicero and Boethius, more than from any others, Gerbert formulated his own ideal of universal man ever seeking for knowledge, and it is this great concept that he tried to impart to his students. Although the rich harvest of his inspiration was not to be realized for another century, in his own time at least one of his students, Adalbold, Bishop of Utrecht, recognized his master's vision, when he addressed him in a letter as 'Pope and philosopher.'[114]

12. Epiphany scene with Christ holding a book, the symbol of wisdom

XIII

The Legacy
of the Schoolmasters

*And they that be wise shall shine as the brightness of the firmament;
and they that turn many to righteousness as the stars forever and ever.*[1]

THE MANY and varied contributions to learning made by the
schoolmasters of the tenth century, from Gregory in the monastery of Einsiedeln in the forest near the Bodensee to the
cosmopolitan Gerbert of Rheims, as they are recorded by history,
indicate that these men were never mere passive links in the chain
of scholars who bridge the chasm between Remigius of Auxerre in
the ninth century and Fulbert of Chartres in the eleventh. The
intellectual and spiritual legacy they left to their students and
their age constitutes a truer measure of their real worth as
teachers than the bare account of their schoolroom achievements.

The most precious bequest of these teachers was the light they
brought to dispel the darkness of their times. Intensely aware of
the heavy losses that both the Church and learning had suffered,
with the consequent spread of ignorance and evil, these men gave
their lives to kindling torches to restore knowledge and virtue.
They themselves spoke little about their efforts to light such
beacons. Instead, like Byrhtferth, they pray for divine illumination; like Bernward, they give their devotion to St. Michael the
Archangel who by his flaming sword overcame the powers of
darkness and evil; or they are like Aelfric who besought his
hearers to learn lest again learning grow cold and fail in his
country as it had not long since; or like Hroswitha who modestly

claimed, "I have inserted in my work some threads torn from the robe of Philosophy, to light up its darkness by nobler material."[2]

More impressive testimony to the effectiveness of the school-masters in dispelling the darkness of ignorance comes from the many writers who shared in the benefits of their great gift of light. In addition to the quotations already given, it is possible to cite more such testimony. They would include a hymn in honor of St. Dunstan where he is hailed as "the true light of the English nation."[3] The chronicle of the abbey of Ely records that Ethelwold "shone forth like a blazing light shedding its brightness upon the people of God."[4] Bishop Oswald is likened to the star of morning gleaming forth out of the darkness "as he illuminated his whole diocese with the rays of his salutary teaching."[5] Abbo's bishop addressed him as "a burning and glowing light that illuminated God's gifts."[6] A poem in honor of Bruno states that "this most brilliant light dispersed the horrible darkness."[7] The biographer of King Robert of France speaks of the wisdom of Gerbert, "which he beamed forth upon the whole world."[8]

By kindling the light of learning, the schoolmasters became the benefactors of all of their people. In the more restricted field of teaching, they made at least three important bequests to scholar-ship: a concept of the teacher as an understanding guide to the young; some innovative methods for presenting the liberal arts; and the libraries which they were instrumental in assembling.

The true significance of these gifts can be appreciated only when they are considered in their place in the history of education. For a thousand years, from the fifth century to the fifteenth, Martianus Capella's great encyclopedia of the liberal arts determined the rigid pattern of education in Europe. In it the author presents Dame Grammar as the typical teacher when he describes her as standing with a whip in her hand tyrannizing over a subdued class of small boys.[9] By a curious irony, however, the tenth century was least influenced by this repellent stereotype, since all the wars, conflagrations, and other disasters that swept over Europe at the end of the ninth century almost destroyed the continuity of learning as many of the books and the teachers disappeared. Then when responsible men of good courage started to rebuild and to recover what they had lost, those who had the ability and the vocation for it were relatively unfettered by Martianus' harsh attitude and inflexible methods.

An ideal for the conduct of these teachers with their pupils was formulated by Ratherius of Verona in his *Praeloquia,* where he advises the teacher to make it his goal to help the student rather than rule over him. More remarkable is his simple maxim: "Choose to be loved rather than to be feared."[10] This is not, however, an invitation to discard discipline, for Ratherius recalls the Biblical proverb, "Whom the Lord loveth, he correcteth," but it is an appeal to the masters to try to teach children not by fear of the rod but for love of the word. Many of the schoolmasters seem to have been guided by some such philosophy of their own devising, for one hears little of whippings. Even Byrhtferth who had difficulties expounding arithmetic to some of his indifferent or lazy pupils speaks in terms of coaxing the boys to learn what they needed so badly. Aelfric appears to have had a very informal relationship with his students as one sees in the *Colloquy* where he jokingly asks them if they would be willing to be flogged if necessary to achieve proficiency in speaking Latin. Odo of Cluny, although he admitted that at times the rod was the only stimulus, preferred to rely upon his wonderful gift of humor to teach his boys.

Ratherius recommends compassion for the weak and untrained pupils, recalling St. Paul's words to the new converts, "Even as babes unto Christ, I have fed you with milk, not meat." Egbert of Liège says that he wrote his auxiliary textbook, the *Fecunda ratis* particularly for the benefit of the frightened little boys who were new to the experience of the classroom.[11] Everaclus expressed his patience with slow learners and encouraged them to ask questions. Aelfric, too, advocated sympathetic treatment for the untried young pupils and almost illiterate priests as he translated the essentials into English. On the other hand, those who were ready for more advanced work were not held back by the less able pupils. Thangmar took his precocious young pupil, Bernward, on his official journeys and taught him as they rode along. In turn, Bernward took his most promising pupils on his journeys to famous cities where they might see great works of art and study them. According to his biographer, Notger of Liège managed the complex problem of teaching both completely inexperienced boys and advanced students, by feeding milk to the very young and solid food to the stronger.[12]

Another Biblical quotation that Ratherius uses in his advice to teachers is Christ's statement to his disciples, "I call you not servants, but friends."[13] The warm and lasting friendships that were formed between master and pupils are most vividly illustrated in numerous letters of Gerbert to his old teachers at Aurillac and again to his former pupils who were teaching in various schools in northern Europe. Years after they had left his school, these disciple-friends felt quite free to write to their old master to ask for his assistance in problems of the sciences or to ask for his diagrams and astronomical instruments. When Abbo left England after only two years, his pupils continued to send him letters and ask for his help. Many of these disciples became the biographers of their old masters; for example, John of Salerno wrote of Odo, Aimoin wrote the life of Abbo, Byrhtferth wrote Oswald's biography, Aelfric wrote that of Ethelwold, Thangmar wrote the life of Bernward, and Richer wrote a full account of Gerbert in his history of France.

The second pedagogical bequest of the schoolmasters was also a complete departure from the rigidity of Martianus Capella's pattern. They devised new methods for teaching the old arts. Notger of Liège, for example, managed a kind of peripatetic school, for he always took a group of students, along with a travelling library and other school equipment, on his episcopal journeys all over Europe. In charge of a chaplain, the boys studied no less than if they had been in a conventional school, keeping a regular schedule, and they also had the advantage of visiting cities of historic interest and seeing some of the most influential men of their time.

Another way in which the teachers showed their imagination was in devising unusual texts. To teach poetry to her pupils Hroswitha wrote plays on inspirational themes from Christian history to replace the unsuitable comedies of Terence.[14] Egbert of Liège composed a reading book of graduated selections from proverbs, fables, Biblical stories, lives of the saints, and local legends, which had the advantage of being suited to the pupils' state of learning and of being germane to their experience.

An innovative teaching method, which would seem entirely logical, but one which the masters had to justify to their superiors, was that of translating instructional texts into the vernacular. In St. Gall, Notker Labeo initiated this unusual procedure when he translated into German the *Sayings of Cato,* the first two books of Martianus Capella, along with a running commentary, the *Consolation of Philosophy* of Boethius, and other texts. Aelfric translated into English the Latin grammar of Priscian and Donatus, large sections of the lives of the saints, and considerable portions of the Bible.

Some of the schoolmasters showed their originality when they endeavored to make the arts of the trivium more understandable by explaining the contents by means of diagrams and charts. The intricacies of rhetoric and dialectic in particular were made clearer by the diagrams of Abbo and Gerbert. Byrhtferth prepared illustrative charts to explain such arithmetical and astronomical phenomena as the seasons, the zodiac, the phases of the moon and the Paschal cycle. More remarkable were the three-dimensional devices brought to the classroom by Gerbert to teach the sciences of the quadrivium. For arithmetic he had an abacus made, and he introduced the Hindu-Arabic numerals for use with it; for geometry he used the astrolabe; in teaching music he employed the monochord and had organs constructed; for astronomy he devised a number of celestial spheres to demonstrate the configuration of the heavens and the arrangement of the planetary system; he went further and invented viewing tubes by which his students could observe celestial phenomena at night.

Finally, these schoolmasters spent great energy in building up libraries for their schools and emphasized their supreme importance for learning. While earlier teachers could take for granted that there would be a library, in the tenth century it was often necessary for them to assemble one. When Odo, for instance, went to the monastery of Baume to teach, he presented the school with one hundred manuscripts, his entire fortune. While Abbo was studying in Paris and in Rheims, he collected what books he could for his monastery at Fleury. When he went to England, he took books for presents, and when he returned he was given other books. Although Fleury had one of the best libraries in Europe, legend has it that when Abbo returned to teach there, he exacted as tuition two books a year from each student.[15] In England Dunstan, with the cooperation of King Edgar, made great efforts to restore the ancient library at Glastonbury, and he succeeded in adding books from many sources. Ethelwold made a generous gift of books to the new monastery of Peterborough; his great love for beautiful books made him give special attention to the scriptorium and the training of monks who produced some famous manuscripts. Bernward, too, collected books on all of his journeys, but he, too, had particular interest in the production of beautifully decorated manuscripts. Bruno took advantage of his ecclesiastical position to visit many libraries and to gather books for his library at Cologne. The most persistent and untiring book collector, however, was Gerbert who gathered a great library at Rheims, at first by securing manuscripts from the many cities he visited, then by sending to numerous libraries asking to have books copied for him. His letters reveal that he sent requests to former teachers, former associates, former students, bishops who had charge of episcopal libraries, and directly to monastic libraries. For this extraordinary humanist-scholar, books were far more than tools for teaching. In one of his letters written to a friend thanking him for some manuscripts of Cicero, Gerbert indicates that for him in his serious troubles the library was truly a "house of healing for the soul,"[16] as he says, "Nothing in human affairs is more preferable to a knowledge of the most distinguished men which assuredly is unfolded in the numerous volumes of their works."[17] Whatever their motive for collecting books—the urgent need for textbooks, the love of beautiful manuscripts, or the comfort and support of the noblest minds of the past—as the result of their efforts the schoolmasters left a gift of incalculable worth to their successors.

The schoolmasters left their heirs truly remarkable material and physical gifts in good schools, with better instruction, more innovative teaching methods, and richer libraries, but one of their most significant benefactions was an intangible one, their concept of the goal of all learning as the attainment of *sapientia,* wisdom. Throughout their lives these men persistently sought after knowledge, *scientia,* not for their own glorification, but that they might pass it on to their disciples. Their object was never simply to reclaim the great accumulation of the learning of the past, but rather to go beyond the secular studies of the seven liberal arts to what Gerbert calls "the art of arts," that is, "the guidance of souls." Apparently many of the masters succeeded in communicating their purpose to their students, for while one or another is characterized as *doctus* or *eruditus,* learned, skilled, or accomplished, more often they are designated as *sapientes,* wise, or *sapientissimi,* endowed with the greatest understanding. Although these men were not philosophers and were not trained in metaphysics, and wrote no treatises on the subject or even made a precise definition of the word, yet they frequently reminded their disciples of the objective of their learning, *sapientia.* Whether they called it holy learning (*sacra eruditio*), sacred wisdom (*sancta sapientia*), or the erudition of salvation (*saluberrima erudito*), they thought of the search for wisdom as a striving for a knowledge of the truth as it is revealed in Scripture and in the doctrines of the Church for the edification and salvation of the Christian.

This ideal of wisdom was, of course, not original with the

schoolmasters but was part of the heritage left them by some of
their teachers of the ninth century. Remigius of Auxerre discusses
sapientia at some length in his commentary on the work of
Martianus Capella.[18] For him, the mastery of the seven liberal arts
led to philosophy which is the love of wisdom and the discernment
of truth. The goal of men's intellectual and spiritual striving must
be *sapientia.* In like manner, men of the eleventh century, receiving
the concept of wisdom from their teachers, adapted it into their
more complex system of thought. Fulbert, the master of the
cathedral school of Chartres, taught that the seven arts are the
handmaids of theology, the queen of the sciences. From the study
of Scripture, the Fathers, Church history, and canon law, one
might hope to come to some idea of the wisdom of God.[19]
However diverse their approaches, both Remigius and Fulbert
were seeking precisely what the scholars of the tenth century
were praying for in the Advent antiphon especially fitting to
them: "O Sapientia, quae ex ore Altissimi prodiisti, attingens a
fine usque ad finem, fortiter suaviterque disponens omnia, veni ad
docendum nos viam prudentiae."[20]

Notes

Abbreviations

used in the Notes and Selected Bibliography

E.E.T.S.	Early English Text Society
M.G.H. SS.	Monumenta Germaniae Historica. Scriptores
P.L.	Patrologia Latina
R.S.	Rolls Series

1. C.Baronius, *Annales ecclesiastici,* ed. A. Theiner (Rouen, 1868), p. 467.

2. H.Waddell (*The Wandering Scholars,* 7th ed. London, 1966, p. 70) coined the phrase to define the status of the tenth century among earlier writers.

3. Inter alia, see H.Waddell, *The Wandering Scholars,* pp. 70-90; R.S.Lopez, *The Tenth Century. How Dark the Dark Ages?* (N.Y., 1959); L. White, "Symposium on the Tenth Century," *Medievalia et Humanistica* IX (1955), pp. 3-29; E.S.Duckett, *Death and Life in the Tenth Century* (Ann Arbor, 1967).

4. R.S.Lopez, "Still another Renaissance?" *American Historical Review* LVII (1951-2), pp. 1-11.

5. J. de Ghellinck, *Le mouvement théologique du XIIe siècle* (Brussels, 1948), p. 47, where he is paraphrasing A.Hauck, *Kirchengeschichte Deutschlands* (Leipzig, 1920), III,322.

6. *Iohannis Scotti Annotationes in Marcianum* (ed. C.E.Lutz, Cambridge, 1939), p. 64. M.T.D'Alverny in "Le symbolisme de la sagesse et le Christ de Saint Dunstan," *Bodleian Library Record* V (1954-6), p. 243, considers this isolated statement in the context of Scotus' total system and equates "philosophy" with Christ.

7. Letter 1 Ad Einhardum (ed. L.Levillan, Paris, 1927, I,p.6).

8. Rodulfus Glaber, *Historiarum libri* II,12 (*P.L.* CXLII, 644).

9. P.Jaffé, "Monumenta Bambergensia," *Bibliotheca rerum Germanicarum* V, 483.

10. For example, Dunstan's biographer likens him to a clever bee flying over the meadows of the sacred and divine volumes gathering nectar. (*Vita Sancti Dunstani auctore B* in W. Stubbs, *Memorials of St. Dunstan* (London, 1874), p. 10. R. S.).

11. *Vita Iohannis abbatis Gorziensis auctore Iohanne abbate S. Arnoulfi* (*M.G.H. SS.* IV, cap. 17, p. 341).

12. *Vita Sancti Udalrici auctore Gerardo* (*P.L.* CXXXV, 1004).

13. *Vita Sancti Abbonis auctore Aimoino monacho* (*P.L.* CXXXIX, 389).

14. For example, in a letter to Odo of Cluny, Fulco recalls that his former

teacher was accustomed "to refresh my thirsting soul." (*Epistola ad Odonem* in M.Marrier, *Bibliotheca Cluniacensis*, Brussels, 1915, p. 114).

15. Anselm, *Gesta episcoporum Leodiensium* (*M.G.H. SS.* VII, 201).

16. Byrhtferth's *Manual*, ed. S.T.Crawford (London, 1919), p. 59. *E.E.T.S.*

17. P.Piper, *Notkers Schriften und seine Schule* (Freiburg and Tübingen, 1882), I,860-1, Letter to Bishop Hugo II of Sitten.

18. *Fecunda ratis*, ed. E.Voight (Halle, 1889).

19. Thangmar, *Vita sancti Bernwardi episcopi* (*M.H.G. SS.* IV, cap. 1, p. 758).

20. W.Stubbs, *Memorials of St. Dunstan, Vita Sancti Dunstani*, p. 49, (London, 1874) R. S.

21. *Vita Odonis* (*P.L.* CXXXIII, 49).

22. C.Leonardi, "Nuove voce poetiche tra seculo IXe e XIe," *Studi Medioevali*, III,2.1 (1961), p. 166.

23. Letter 74 (*The Letters of Gerbert*, ed. H.P.Lattin, N.Y., 1961, p. 113).

24. Piper, *Notkers Schriften*, p. 859.

25. St. Odo of Cluny, for example, when asked by some of the monks at Tours to make an epitome of St. Gregory's *Moralia*, was very reluctant to do this until he was warned by a vision of the great Father himself. His biographer, John of Salerno, says, "He did not undertake this work out of arrogance, but by the Lord's disposal, that the light which was hidden under a measure should be set on a hill-top." (G.Sitwell, *St. Odo of Cluny*, London, 1958, p. 22).

26. Latin preface to Aelfric's *Grammar*, translated by C.L.White, *Aelfric* (New Haven, 1898), p. 119.

27. *Vita Mahthildis reginae* (*M.G.H. SS.* IV, 289).

28. *Aelfric's Lives of the Saints*, ed. W.W.Skeat (London, 1881) *Nativitas Domini nostri Iesu Christi*, lines 36,75-6,240-1, pp. 13,15,25.

29. Now in the Bodleian Library, it is MS. Auct. F. 4.32 (2176). It has been fully discussed by R.W.Hunt in *Saint Dunstan's Classbook from Glastonbury* (Amsterdam, 1961).

30. The symbolism has been discussed by M.T.D'Alverny, "Le symbolisme," *Bodleian Library Record* V (1954-6), 241-2.

Notes to Chapter II

1. Peter the Venerable, *Epistola* 17, Lib. VI. Quoted in M.Marrier, *Bibliotheca Cluniacensis* (Brussels and Paris, 1915), p. 58.

2. J. Trithemius, *De scriptoribus ecclesiasticis* CCLXXXV, in J.A.Fabricius, *Bibliotheca ecclesiastica* (Hamburg, 1718) 76.

3. *Vita Odonis* by John of Salerno (*P.L.* CXXXIII, 52). A translation of the *Life* is given by G.Sitwell, *St. Odo of Cluny* (N.Y., 1958), pp. 3-87.

4. Ibid.

5. Ibid.

6. *P.L.* CXXXIII, 517-638.

7. *Vita,* 44-46.

8. *Vita,* 44.

9 *Vita,* 43.

10. Early testimonials to the life of Odo have been assembled by M.Marrier, *Bibliotheca,* pp. 55-62.

11. *Magister scholae* is the phrase normally used to indicate a schoolmaster, but *praeceptor* and *scholasticus* are also found.

12. *Vita,* 48.

13. *Vita,* 52.

14. The text is given in *P.L.* CXXXIII, 109-512.

15. The text was edited by A. Swoboda (Leipzig, 1900).

16. *P.L.* CXXXIII, 639-705. A translation is given in Sitwell's *St. Odo,* pp. 90-180.

17. *P.L.* CXXXIII, 710-752.

18. *P.L.* CXXXIII, 513-516.

19. Sigebertus Gemblacensis, *Chronicon* for the year 898 (*P.L.* CLX, 173) and *Liber de scriptoribus ecclesiasticis* cap. cxxiv (*P.L.* CLX, 573).

20. *P.L.* CXXXIII, 755-816.

21. See Sitwell, *St. Odo,* p. xxvi.

22. M.Prou, *Raoul Glaber, Les cinque livres de ses Histoires* (Paris, 1886) III,18, p. 67.

23. Quoted in Marrier, *Bibliotheca,* p. 57.

24. *Vita,* 49.

25. *Vita,* 51.

26. *Vita,* 63.

27. John says (*Vita,* 63), "Locutio vero sua prae nimis gaudio ridere nos cogebat."

28. *Vita,* 75.

29. *Collationes* I,3 (*P.L.* CXXXIII, 522).

30. *Vita,* 72-73.

31. Ordericus Vitalis, who lived in the twelfth century, claims that two thousand monasteries were reformed by Odo and the monks of Cluny. P. Schmitz (*Histoire de l'Ordre de Saint-Benoît,* Maredsous, 1948, I, 145) believes that the number 1450 would be closer to the facts.

Peter the Venerable, writing about 1140, aptly summarizes the achievement of Odo: "Veniat post magnum Benedictum et eius discipulum Maurum summus Ordinis Monastici in Gallia reparator, Odo: Odo, inquam, primus Cluniacensis Ordinis Pater, qui emortuum iam et pene ubique septultum Monastici propositi fervorem resuscitare summo conamine agressus est." *Epistolae* VI,17, quoted in Marrier, *Bibliotheca,* p.58.

32. Reinerus, *Vita Everacli, M.G.H. SS.* XX,562.

33. The initial interest of the founders of the northern reform movement was asceticism and the solitary life rather than community life, so the spiritual development of the monk was chiefly emphasized. In government, unlike the

Cluniac monasteries which sought uniformity, the northern houses maintained their individual ways; they were satisfied to remain under the patronage of the king or local noble rather than insisting upon independence of all save the pope.

34. The only contemporary biography of Gerard was lost, but it was used by an unknown monk in his *Vita Gerardi abbatis Broniensis* written about 1045. See *M.G.H. SS.* XV.2, 564-673. A modern analysis of the *Vita* is that of U.Berlière, "Etude sur la Vita Gerardi Broniensis," *Revue Bénédictine* IX (1872), 157-172,

35. A biography of John was written by his friend, John, the abbot of St. Arnoul of Metz. See *M.G.H., SS.* IV, 335-377. The abbot calls John (p. 345) "second to none in his knowledge of both secular and religious studies in his time."

36. A monk of the abbey of St. Laurent of Liège, Reinerus, in the twelfth century, wrote the biography of Everaclus (*M.G.H., SS.* 561-565). References are to this text.

37. Variants of the name include: Ebrachar, Everarchus, Euraclus, Ever-acrus, Evracher, and Heraclius.

38. "Epistola B ad Aethelgarum archiepiscopum," in W.Stubbs, *Memorials of St. Dunstan* (London, 1874), pp. 385-388. *R.S.*

39. These include: Anselm, *Gesta episcoporum Leodiensium* (*M.G.H., SS.* VII, 201-202), Rupertus, *Chronicon Sancti Laurentii Leodiensis* (*M.G.H., SS.* VIII, 262-264), and Aegidius Aureaevallensis, *Gesta episcoporum Leodiensium* (*M.G.H., SS.* XXV, 53-57).

40. Reinerus was chiefly interested in presenting Everaclus as the founder of the abbey of St. Laurent. See H.Silvestre, "Notes sur la 'Vita Evracli' de Renier de Saint-Laurent." *Revue d'histoire ecclésiastique* XLIV (1949), 30-86.

41. For the life of Ratherius, see E.S.Duckett, *Death and Life in the Tenth Century* (Ann Arbor, 1967), pp. 309-313.

42. Reinerus (*Vita,* 562) says, "Tantam in divinis aeque et humanis assecutus est scientiam, ut summis par esse philosophis jure censeretur, praesertim cum venustatem corporis mores etiam inaurarent splendidi, et juxta Salomonem in facie luceret sapientia." Rupertus (*Chronicon,* 262) testifies, "Omnibus scholarum studiis ita perfecte eruditus extitit, ut suis temporibus par ei nullatenus inveniri potuerit."

43. *Vita,* 562. He quotes four lines from Horace, *Ep.* I.2.32-37.

44. *Vita,* 562: "exultans in gaudio, lucernam talem poni super aecclesiae Leodiensis candelabrum."

45. The author of the *Vita Balderici* (*M.G.H., SS.* IV, 731) gives Everaclus credit for being the first to restore learning and religion to Liège.

46. J.Chapeauville, *Gesta pontificum Tungriensium* (Liège, 1612) I, 190-191. See H.Silvestre, "Comment on rédigeait une lettre au Xe siècle, *Le Moyen Age* LVIII (1952), 4-6. The humorous reference to discipline is taken from Juvenal, *Sat.* I.15 and Persuis, *Sat.* V.40; it may indicate that Everaclus studied the satirists under Ratherius.

47. Anselm, *Gesta* 201.

48. *Vita* 563; Anselm, *Gesta* 202.
50. *Vita* 565.
51. *Daniel* XII.3.

Notes to Chapter III

1. *Vita Sancti Dunstani auctore B* in W.Stubbs, *Memorials of St. Dunstan* (London, 1874), pp. 23-25. R. S. Dom David Knowles (*The Monastic Order in England,* Cambridge, 1950, p. 38) calls this a "decisive moment in the history of religion in England."

2. *Vita Sancti Dunstani auctore Willelmo Malmesbiriensi* in Stubbs, *Memorials,* p. 290.

3. *Vita—B,* Stubbs, *Memorials,* p. 37.

4. Historia Rameseiensis in *Chronicon Abbatiae Rameseiensis,* ed. W.D.Macray (London, 1886), p. 25.*R.S.*

5. Two biographies were written within twenty-five years after Dunstan's death. The first, by a Saxon priest who identifies himself only as "B," was written about the year 1000; the second, by Adelard, a monk of Blandinium, was written before 1011. Three more *Vitae* written in the eleventh and twelfth centuries are more critical than the early ones. They are the works of Osbern, Eadmer, and William of Malmesbury. All of these texts are printed in Stubbs, *Memorials.* I shall follow the *Vita* by "B" unless otherwise indicated.

6. The *Vita S.Aethelwoldi* by Aelfric, written about 1006, is published in *Chronicon Monasterii de Abingdon,* ed. J.Stevenson (London, 1858) II, 255-266. R. S. See D.J.V.Fisher, "The Early Biographers of St. Ethelwold," in *English Historical Review* LXVII (1952), 381-391.

7. The *Vita Sancti Oswaldi auctore anonymo,* written about 1005, is edited by J.Raine in his *Historians of the Church of York and Its Archbishops* (London, 1879), I, 399-475. *R.S.*

8. D.Knowles, *The Religious Houses of Medieval England* (London, 1940), p. 15, says, "The acorn, the seed of the new birth that was to grow into a majestic oak, was planted by a single hand, that of Dunstan."

9. The fullest account of Dunstan's studies with the Irish monks is found in the *Vita* of William of Malmesbury, Stubbs, *Memorials,* pp. 256-257.

10. *Vita auctore Osberno,* Stubbs, *Memorials,* p. 78.

11. Knowles, *The Monastic Order,* p. 533. Two large bells said to have been made by Dunstan were placed in the church at Abingdon. See Stevenson, *Chronicon,* I, 345.

12. *Vita—B,* Stubbs, *Memorials,* 25, where he is called "the first abbot of the English nation."

13. Stubbs, *Memorials*, p. 272.

14. They are: Oxon. Auct. F.4.32 (2176); Hatton 30 (S.C. 4076); and Hatton 42 (S.C. 4117). See R.W.Hunt, *Saint Dunstan's Classbook from Glastonbury* (Amsterdam, 1961), pp. xv-xvi. J.W.Thompson in *The Medieval Library* (Chicago, 1939) p. 123, notes several more manuscripts from Canterbury in Dunstan's time, now in English libraries.

15. See chapter I, pp. 10-11.

16. In a letter to Dunstan by an unidentified writer, the archbishop is called "Doctorum ductor sapiens tu vir sapientum," (Stubbs, *Memorials*, p. 371.) Another correspondent likens Dunstan to Minerva for his wisdom and to Apollo for his musical ability. (Stubbs, *Memorials*, p. 373). The learned Abbo of Fleury composed for Dunstan two acrostic poems, more ingenious than meritorious. (Stubbs, *Memorials*, pp. 410,411).

17. *Willelmi Malmesbiriensis Monachi Gesta pontificum Anglorum*, ed. N.E.S.A. Hamilton (London, 1870) p. 196.

18. T.Hearne, *Joannis Glastoniensis, Chronica* (Oxford, 1726), II, pp. 423-444. Of the 264 volumes listed 124 are qualified as "vetusti," "vetustissimi," "legibiles," and "inutiles," which may indicate that they survived the fire which destroyed the monastery in 1184.

19. Knowles, *The Religious Houses*, p. 18.

20. *Vita—B* (Stubbs, *Memorials*, pp. 41 and 43). In Eadmer's *Vita* (Stubbs, *Memorials*, p. 206) the story is told that in a dream he heard the music of the chant *Kyrie rex splendens*, which was later sung on Dunstan's feast day.

21. "Ideoque omnis haec Anglica terra doctrina ejus sancta repleta est fulgens coram Deo et hominibus sicut sol et luna." *Vita-B* (Stubbs, *Memorials*, p. 50).

22. *Vita Sancti Dunstani, auctore Willelmo Malmesbiriensi*, in W.Stubbs, *Memorials*, pp. 272-273.

23. *Vita S. Aethelwoldi episcopi Wintoniensis, auctore Aelfrico*, ed. J.Stevenson (London, 1858) in *Chronicon Monasterii de Abingdon*, II, 255-266. This biography was used in the *Historia Monasterii de Abingdon*, Book II. See *Chronicon*, I, 121-124, 343-349. Aelfric's biography is the basis of my account.

24. *P.L.* CXXXVII. 82-107. See J. Armitage Robinson, *The Times of St. Dunstan* (Oxford, 1923) pp. 105-108.

25. *Vita Oswaldi*, in J.Raine, *Historians of the Church of York* (London, 1877) I, 426-427.

26. *Chronicon* I, 344-345 and II, 277-278.

27. *Liber Eliensis*, ed. D.J.Stewart (London, 1848) II, p. 153. The Chronicle relates that King Edgar gave him the manor of Suthburne on the condition that he translate the *Rule*.

28. *Liber Eliensis* II, 105-108.

29. W.Dugdale, *Monasticon Anglicanun* (London, 1849) I, 382.

30. See above, p. 25. Ethelwold uses a number of Greek words, for example, in the *Benedictional* he uses "Theophania" for Epiphany.

31. This volume, now Additional MS 49598, was in the library of the Duke of

Devonshire until 1957. It is described by F. Wormald in *The Benedictional of St. Ethelwold* (London, 1959) and eight of the miniatures are reproduced. The whole manuscript has been reproduced in facsimile by G.F.Warner and H.A.Wilson (Oxford, 1910).

32. Ethelwold's constant association with books is illustrated by a very charming episode that occurred in his old age. Aelfric says, "It happened that as the bishop was reading at night, in spite of his efforts to watch, he fell asleep, and the lighted candle fell on the page, and burnt it as it lay upon it, until a brother coming in took the burning candle off the book, and found the sparks lying on many of the lines inside the book, and blowing these out he found the page uninjured." (S.H.Gem, *An Anglo-Saxon Abbot, Aelfric of Eynsham,* Edinburgh, 1912, p. 179.)

33. *Vita Sancti Oswaldi, auctore anonymo,* in J. Raine, *Historians of the Church of York* (London, 1879) I, 399.

34. The biography may well have been written by Byrhtferth, the most outstanding scholar of Ramsey. E. S. Duckett, *Saint Dunstan of Canterbury* (N.Y., 1955) p. 237, reviews the literature on the authorship. I follow this biography except where otherwise noted.

35. In *Chronicon Abbatiae Rameseiensis,* ed. W. D. Macray (London, 1886), pp. 21-51. Four other accounts of the life of Oswald are edited by Raine, *Historians* II, 1-87. Of these only the *Vita* by Eadmer of Canterbury in the early twelfth century adds anything of significance to the anonymous *Life.*

36. This information is supplied by Eadmer, *Life,* in *Historians* II, 5-6. It also is given in the *Historia Rameseiensis,* in *Chronicon,* p. 21.

37. Frithegode seems to have known Greek if one can judge by the presence of many Greek words in his metrical *Life of St. Wilfrid* (*Historians* I, 105-159). William of Malmesbury (*Gesta pontificum Anglorum,* p. 22) reports that Frithegode hated Latin and loved Greek so that he frequently used Greek words.

38. For Byrhtferth, see below, chapter V.

39. Harley MS 2904.

40. Charles Niver has discussed this manuscript in an article, "The Psalter in the British Museum, Harley 2904," in *Medieval Studies in Memory of A. Kingsley Porter* (Cambridge, 1939), II, 667-687.

41. Abbo will be treated more fully in chapter IV. The main source of his life is Aimoin of Fleury which is published in *P.L.* CXXXIX, 375-582.

42. A full description of the ceremony is given in the anonymous *Life* of Oswald (*Historians* I, 436-38).

43. See *Life,* p. 425.

44. The Latin text and translation are given by T. Symons, *Regularis Concordia* (N.Y., 1953).

45. The document is anonymous, but it is generally agreed that the actual composition was made by Ethelwold. See T. Symons, *Concordia,* pp. li and lii, and Duckett, *Saint Dunstan,* pp. 182-183.

46. It is generally accepted that during this period forty-eight religious houses were restored, eight of which were for nuns. (Stubbs, *Memorials,* 214).

47. *Lives of the Saints,* ed. W.W.Skeat (London, 1881) XXI, 444-447 (Vol.I,p.469) It continues (lines 457-462):

> At that time there were also worthy bishops,
> Dunstan, the resolute, in the archbishopric,
> and Aethelwold the venerable, and others like them;
> but Dunstan and Aethelwold were chosen of God;
> and they, most of all, exhorted men to do God's will,
> and advanced everything good, to the pleasure of God.

48. Knowles, *The Monastic Order in England* (Cambridge, 1950) p. 47.

Notes to Chapter IV

1. Abbo, *Praefatio Commentarii in Cyclum Victorii* (*P.L.* CXXXIX, 571). Most of the works of Abbo are edited in *P. L.* CXXXIX, 375-582. The many references to this work will be indicated in the text by the column number.

2. C.Cuissard, *Catalogue générale des Manuscrits des Bibliothèques de France. Orléans* (Paris, 1889), MS 127, vol. XII, 51, and L.Delisle, "Mémoire sur d'anciens sacramentaires", *Mémoires de l'Institut National de France* (Paris, 1886) pp. 211-218.

3. P.Cousin, *Abbon de Fleury-sur-Loire* (Paris, 1953) p. 65,n. 12, and C.Niver, "The Psalter in the British Museum, Harley 2904," in *Medieval Studies in Memory of A. Kingsley Porter* (Cambridge, 1939) II, 678-684.

4. M.Prou and A. Vidier, *Recueil des Chartes de l'Abbaye de Saint-Benoît-sur-Loire* (Paris, 1900-7) I, 187.

5. Odolricus is quoted in the account of the Council of Limoges (1031). See J.Mansi, *Sacrorum Conciliorum nova et amplissima Collectio* (Venice, 1774) XIX, 511.

6. A later biographer, J. Du Bois-Oliver (*Floriacesis vetus Biblioteca,* Fleury, 1605, p. 242), states, without revealing his source, that there were over five thousand students in Abbo's school, an estimate that is grossly exaggerated. He also says that each student gave two manuscripts a year for his tuition. This would help to account for the unusually fine library at the abbey.

7. See above, chapter III, pp. 37-38.

8. *Miracula Sancti Benedicti* of Andreus of Fleury, Book VII, chap. XIII, p. 270, ed. of E.de Certain (Paris, 1858).

9. J.W.Thomson, *The Medieval Library* (Chicago, 1939) pp. 61; 227-230. E.K.Rand has described one of the surviving manuscripts which must have served as a kind of teaching manual. See "A *Vademecum* of Liberal Culture in a Manuscript of Fleury," *Philological Quarterly* I(1922), 258-278.

10. Gerbert, Letter 92, ed. H.P.Lattin (N.Y., 1961), p. 127.

11. The text of the letter is given in Stubbs, *Memorials,* pp. 376-377. The fire occurred in 974.

12. P.Cousin, *Abbon,* appendix V, pp. 223-225.

13. P.Cousin, *Abbon,* appendix IV, pp. 218-222.

14. For a discussion of the contents see O.Funke, *Über die 'Quaestiones Grammaticales' des Abbo Floriacensis* (Halle, 1914).

15. This passage, which in the *Patrologia* (529) is badly corrupted, has been emended by H.Bradley in an article "On the Text of Abbo of Fleury's *Quaestiones Grammaticales* (*Proceedings of the British Academy,* 1921-1923, p. 176) as follows: "Sed aspirationes bene vos angli pervidere potestis, qui pro Θ frequentius þ scribitis, sicut pro digamma ƿ."

16. A.Van de Vyver, "Les oeuvres inédites d'Abbon de Fleury," *Revue Bénédictine* XLVII (1935), 133.

17. Op. cit. 140-150.

18. These three works are cited in Van de Vyver, 140-141.

19. Byrhtferth's *Manual,* ed. S.J.Crawford (London, 1929) pp. 232-233.

20. Parts of the commentary have been published by W.von Christ, "Über das argumentum calculandi des Victorius und dessen Commentar," *Sitzungsberichte der Königl. bayer. Akademie der Wissenschaften zu München* I (1863), 138-152. Only the Introduction is given in *P.L.* CXXXIX, 571.

21. For this interesting phenomenon which has been called his "shorthand," see W.Schmitz, "Zum mittelalterlichen Unterrichten in den tironischen Noten," *Neues Archiv* XXIII (1898), 260-262 and L.Auvray, "Deux manuscrits de Fleury-sur-Loire," *Annales de la Société historique et archéologique de Gâtinais* VII (1889), 50.

22. See Van de Vyver, 15-154.

23. The tables printed with the works of Bede (*P.L.* XC, 825-858) may be the work of Abbo.

24. *P.L.* XC, 859-878.

25. Only one has been published. See P.Varin, "Lettre critique d'Abbon de Fleury sur les cycles dionysiaques," *Bulletin du Comité des travaux historiques et scientifiques* I (1849), 115-127.

26. The dedicatory letter to the *Passio S.Aedmundi* (507-508) is addressed to Dunstan, and three poems were written to him (Stubbs, *Memorials,* pp. 410-412).

27. In Ep. 2 (*P.L.* CXLI, 190) he calls Abbo "most beloved father" and speaks of his "holy friendship."

28. These works are printed in *P.L.* CXXXIX, 797-870.

29. In the preface to the *Vita* (387-388), Aimoin says to Herveus, "You were beloved of him and your devotion proves that you loved him." He also speaks of Abbo as the "nourisher" of both Herveus and himself. Abbo's Letter V (423) is directed to the monks of St. Martin and especially to Herveus.

30. P.Cousin, *Abbon,* pp. 99-104.

31. See above, note 5.

32. F.M.Warren, "Constantine of Fleury," *Transactions of the Connecticut Academy of Arts and Sciences* XV (1909), 285-292.

33. P.Ewald, "The Life of Gauzelin by André of Fleury," *Neues Archiv* III (1878), 351-385.

34. See below, chapter V.

35. See *Histoire litéraire* VII, 575-588.

36. Op. cit.VII, 295-299 and P.Cousin, *Abbon,* p. 202.

37. Rodulfus Glaber gives a full account in his *Historiae* III,ll (ed. M.Prou, Paris, 1886, pp. 60-61). The official letter from Fleury on the assassination is given in *P.L.* CXXXIX, 417-418.

38. L.Bethmann, "Handschriften der Stadtbibliothek zu S. Gallen," *Neues Archiv* IX (1847), 588-589. This is MS 337.

Notes to Chapter V

1. *Byrhtferth's Manual* edited by S.J. Crawford (London, 1929) *E.E.T.S.* 177 p. 59. All references in the text will be to the modern English translation in this edition.

2. *Vita sancti Oswaldi auctore anonymo* in J.Raine, *Historians of the Church of York and Its Archbishops* (London, 1879), I, 399-475. *R.S.* See above, chapter III.

3. S.J.Crawford, *Byrhtferth of Ramsey and the Anonymous Life of St. Oswald* in *Speculum Religionis* (Oxford, 1929) pp. 99-111. I follow his arguments for Byrhtferth's authorship.

4. This conclusion is not universally accepted. See J. Armitage Robinson, "Byrhtferth and the Life of St. Oswald," *Journal of Theological Studies* XXXI (1930), 35-42, and D. J. Fisher, "The Anti-Monastic Reaction in the Reign of Edward the Martyr," *Cambridge Historical Journal* X (1952), 258-259.

5. F.M. Stenton, *Anglo-Saxon England* (Oxford, 1943) p. 390.

6. C. and D. Singer, "Byrhtferth's Diagram," *Bodleian Quarterly Record* II (1917), 47-51, and C. and D. Singer, "An Unrecognized Anglo-Saxon Medical Text," *Annals of Medical History* III.2 (1921), 136-149.

7. G. F. Forsey, "Byrhtferth's Preface," *Speculum* III (1928), 505-522, and H. Henel, "Byrhthferth's *Preface:* The Epilogue of his Manual?" *Speculum* XVIII (1943), 288-302.

8. *Manual* p. 157 footnote.

9. See the edition of R.Ewald (*M.G.H., Auctores Antiquissimi* XV), pp. 353-354.

10. It has been suggested that the second work is actually the *Manual.* See R.Steele, "Review of Crawford: *Byrhtferth's Manual* in *Modern Language Review* XXVI (1931), 351-352.

11. They are published in *P.L.* XC, as scholia to the following works of Bede:

188-254 *De natura rerum;* 297-518 *De temporum ratione;* 685-690 *De loquela per gestum digitorum;* 699-702 *De ratione unciarum.* See C.W.Jones, "The Byrhtferth Glosses," *Medium Aevum* VII (1938), 81-97, and C.W.Jones, *Bedae Pseudepigrapha* (London, 1939), 5-35.

12. W.Stubbs, *Memorials of St. Dunstan* (London, 1874) ix-xxx; text 3-52.*R.S.*

13. *Historia Rameseiensis,* p. 48 in *Chronicon Abbatiae Rameseiensis* ed. W.D.Macray (London, 1886). *R.S.* The episode of the bells and the sequel is related on pp. 112-114, 127-128, 147, 159-160.

Notes to Chapter VI

1. *Homilies of Aelfric,* ed. B. Thorpe (London, 1846) II, 537.

2. J. Hurt in his study of Aelfric, calls him "teacher . . . of the English nation itself." (*Aelfric,* N.Y., 1972, p. 136). The author very successfully defends the thesis that all of Aelfric's works fit into a carefully planned program of education.

3. See Aelfric's preface to Genesis in S.J.Crawford, *The Old English Version of the Heptateuch* (London, 1922) p. 76. *E.E.T.S.* 160.

4. In a number of places he speaks of himself as Ethelwold's pupil: see the preface to his *Grammar* (ed. J. Zupitza, Berlin, 1880, p.l), the Latin preface to his *Homilies* (I.1), the Latin preface to his abridgment of the *De consuetudine monachorum* of Ethelwold (M.Bateson in *Obedientiaries of St. Swithin's Priory, Winchester,* ed. G.W.Kitchin, London, 1892, Appendix VII. p. 175.

5. Hurt, *Aelfric,* p. 31.

6. The English preface to the *Homilies* I,7.9. He considered his mission as one directed by God, as he continues, "Very many I know in this country more learned than I am, but God manifests His wonders through whom He will."

7. There are two series, the first written in 989 and the second in 992. They were intended to be read in alternate years, as he specifies in the preface to the second series (p.3).

8. *Homilies* I, Latin preface, translated by S.H.Gem in *An Anglo-Saxon Abbot* (Edinburgh, 1912), pp. 112-113.

9. Gem, p. 113.

10. *Homilies* II, 447.

11. Ibid.

12. *Homilies* II, 371. In several other places Aelfric mentions this idea, for example, in the preface to *Homilies* I,3, he says, "Men have need of good instruction, especially at this time, which is the ending of this world." In *Homilies* I, 477, he calls his contemporaries "the endmen of this world."

13. *Homilies* II, 597-601.

14. *Homilies* II, 461.

15. *Homilies* II, 595.

16. *Homilies* II, 321.

17. *Homilies* II, 537.

18. *Homilies* II, 531.

19. *Homilies* II, 343.

20. *Homilies* II, 533.

21. *Aelfric's Lives of the Saints,* ed. W.W.Skeat (London, 1881). *E.E.T.S.* 76, 82, 94, 114.

22. These include St. Cuthbert, St. Alban, St. Oswald, St. Etheldreda, St. Swithin, and St. Edmund whose biography is largely derived from Abbo's account, as Aelfric states. Cf. II,315.

23. See the preface to I,3.

24. *Lives* I, 337-367.

25. Here the usual seven sins are augmented by an eighth, sorrow, which has its counterpart as spiritual joy among the virtues.

26. See the preface to I,3.

27. Edited by A.Napier, *Wulfstan* (Berlin, 1883), pp. 104-107. The subject is also treated in *Homilies* I,365-383.

28. Edited by R.Morris, *Old English Homilies* (London, 1848), first series, part II, pp. 101-118. E.E.T.S. 29. The twelve abuses are again pointed out in the *Lives* I,291-293.

29. Edited by H.Henel, *Aelfric's De temporibus anni* (London, 1942) E.E.T.S. 213. There is an English translation in O. Cockayne, *Leechdoms, Wortcunning, and Starcraft* (London, 1866), III, 231-281. *R.S.*

30. *Homilies* II,321.

31. Edited by B.Thorpe, *Ancient Laws and Institutes of England* (London, 1840), pp. 441-451.

32. Ibid. p. 445.

33. Ibid. p. 450.

34. Ibid. p. 461.

35. Edited by G.W.Kitchin in M. Bateson, *Obedientiaries of St. Swithin's Priory, Winchester* (London, 1892) Appendix VII, 174-198.

36. Edited by J. Stevenson, "Vita S. Aethelwoldi, Episcopi Wintoniensis auctore Aelfrico", in *Chronicon Monasterii de Abingdon* (London, 1858) II, Appendix I, 255-260. *R.S.*

37. Edited by H.W.Norman, *The Anglo-Saxon Version of the Hexameron of St. Basil* (London, 1849), pp. 31-57. The Latin text has been edited by P. Lehmann, "Die Admonitio S.Basilii ad filium spiritualem," *Sitzungsberichte der Bayerischen Akademie der Wissenschaften,* Phil. Hist. Klasse (1955), pp. 3-63.

38. Norman, pp. 33-35.

39. *Homilies* II, 447-461.

40. *Lives* I, 384-413.

41. *Lives* II, 66-121.

42. *Homilies* II, 594.

43. Edited by S.J.Crawford, *The Old English Version of the Heptateuch, Aelfric's Treatise on the Old and New Testament and his Preface to Genesis* (London, 1922), pp. 81-149. *E.E.T.S.* 160.

44. Ibid. pp. 337-477.

45. Ibid. pp. 401-414.

46. Edited by B.Assmann, "Abt Aelfric's Angelsächsische Bearbeitung des Buches Esther," *Anglia* IX (1886), 25-38.

47. Edited by B.Assmann, "Abt Aelfric's Angelsächsische Homilie über das Buch Judith," *Anglia* X (1888) 76-104.

48. S.J.Crawford, Op. cit., pp. 416-417. Translated by D.Whitlock, *English Historical Documents* (London, 1955), I, 954.

49. Edited by G.E.MacLean, "Aelfric's Version of *Alcuini Interrogationes Sigewulfi in Genesin,*" *Anglia* VII (1884), 1-59.

50. Edited by S.J.Crawford, Op. cit. pp. 15-75.

51. Edited by H.W.Norman, *The Anglo-Saxon Version of the Hexameron of St. Basil,* pp. 1-29.

52. Edited by A. Napier, *Wulfstan,* pp. 56-60.

53. *Homilies* I, 311-329.

54. Edited by J. Zupitza, *Aelfrics Grammatik und Glossar* (Berlin, 1880), pp. 1-196.

55. Preface translated by C.L.White, *Aelfric,* (New Haven, 1898), p. 119.

56. English preface to the *Grammar,* Zupitza p.3.

57. Zupitza, pp. 297-322.

58. Edited by G.M.Garmonsway, *Aelfric's Colloquy* (London, 1947). English translation in Gem, pp. 183-195. References to this translation are indicated in the text.

59. See introduction by W.M.Lindsay in W.H.Stevenson, *Early Scholastic Colloquies* (Anecdota Oxoniensia, Mediaeval and Modern Series, pt. 15) pp. v-vi, and in *The Anglo-Saxons,* ed. P.Clemoes (London, 1959), G.N.Garmonsway, "The Development of the Colloquy" pp. 251-253.

60. O.Cockayne, *Leechdoms,* I,lviii.

61. Translated in C.L.White, p. 119.

62. Preface to the *Grammar,* Zupitza, p. 3.

63. Preface to *Homilies* I, 9; preface to *Homilies* II, 3; preface to *Lives* I, 7; end of *On the Old and New Testament,* p. 75; end of preface to *Grammar* p. 3.

64. Edited by S.J.Crawford, Op. cit. p. 74.

65. For example, of the eight manuscripts of the *De temporibus anni,* seven were written before the Conquest. See H.Henel, *Aelfric's De temporibus anni* pp. ix-xxxix.

66. Skeat (*Lives* II, pp. vii-xxii) lists eighteen manuscripts that have some or all of the Lives: Zupitza (*Grammar,* Vorwort) cites fifteen manuscripts of the *Grammar;* Garmonsway (*Colloquy,* p. 1) cites four manuscripts of the *Colloquium.*

Notes to Chapter VII

1. E. Dümmler and H.Wartmann, "St. Galler Todtenbuch und Ver-brüderung, *Mittheilungen zur vaterländischen Geschichte* XI (1869), 45.

2. J.Egli, "Der *Liber Benedictionum* Ekkeharts IV," *Mittheilungen zur vaterländischen Geschichte* XXXI (1909), 405: *Varia* 14, lines 1-4: Epitaphium quatuor scolarum magistris aeque tumulatis.

3. See I.von Arx, "Ekkehard IV, Casuum S.Galli Continuatio" II, cap. 4 (*M.G.H. SS* II,155) for the year 1022: "Henricus . . . victor ediit in Germaniam. Pestilentia in exercitu orta, multos extinxit . . . Notkerus quoque magister et alii praestantes fratres apud sanctum Gallum decesserunt."

4. *Epitaphium,* lines 7-8.

5. P.G.Meier, "Geschichte der Schule von St.Gallen im Mittelalter," *Jahrbuch für Schweizerische Geschichte* X (1885), 89. The end of intellectual activity at St. Gall came dramatically in 1034 when Conrad II installed Nortpert as abbot and forced the abbey to adopt the Cluniac Reform.

6. J.M.Clark in *The Abbey of St. Gall as a Center of Literature and Art* (Cambridge, 1926), pp. 8-14, names Iso (d. 871), Ratpert, Moengal, Ekkehard I, Notker Balbulus, Tuitilo, Gerald, Ekkehard II, and Burchard I as distinguished predecessors of Notker III.

7. É.Lesne, *Les Écoles de la fin du VIIIᵉ siècle à la fin du XIIᵉ* (Lille, 1940), p. 406: "L'école de Saint-Gall atteint l'apogée au temps où, de l'an 1000 environ a sa mort en 1022, Notker Labeo l'a dirigée."

8. This information is found in a note written in a fourteenth-century hand on folio 246 of codex 393 of St. Gall at the end of Ekkehard's verses 'Ad picturas claustri Sancti Galli." They are printed in Egli, v,note 1:

> Balbus erat Notker, piperis granum fuit alter;
> Tercius hic labio datus est agnomine lato;
> Pectore mandatum gestans labio quoque latum,
> Lacior hinc labio puto nemo videbitur illo.
> Ecce favos labio qua stillat tibi isto.

9. The date of his birth is determined by a reference to his death in 1022 in a gloss on Ekkehard's poem XLIV "Item de aliis sincellitis amborum," line 73, where he is called "septuagenarius." Egli, p.232.

10. Notker wsa also a cousin to Ekkehard III and Abbot Burchard II. See G.Meyer von Knonau "St. Gallische Geschichtsquellen," *Mittheilungen zur vaterländischen Geschichte* XVI (1887), 290, for a notice of the four cousins, nephews of Ekkehard I, who came to St. Gall.

11. E. Dümmler, *Das Formelbuch des Bischofs Salomo III von Konstanz* (Leipzig, 1857).

12. W.H.Harster, *Ualtheri Spirensis Vita et Passio Christophori Martyris* (Munich, 1878), pp. 15-35: "Incipit primus libellus de studio poetae, qui et scholasticus." All of the books mentioned except the Latin *Iliad* were used at St. Gall.

13. Harster, pp. 22-23, lines 93-113.

14. Harster, pp. 23-33, lines 114-223.

15.. Egli, pp. 1-439.

16. Egli, p. 279. A gloss on LIX headed "Dictamen debitum magistro," reads: "Hoc et cetera que scripsi, ipse scribi jussit in cartis suis, ut iuvenes nostros in id ipsum adortarer."

17. Egli, pp. 206-217, XL-XLII: "Confutatio rhetoricae (dialecticae, grammaticae) in facie ecclesiae et sanctorum."

18. Egli, pp. 393-397, *Varia* 5: "Notkero magistro pro pace et solito scolarium otio in die post Epiphaniam."

19. It is recorded that when the emperor, Conrad I, visited the abbey in 911, he instituted as another vacation a three-day holiday to be observed every year with special privileges for the boys. (*Ekkeharti (IV) Casus sancti Galli,* cap. 16, edited by G.Meyer von Knonau, *Mittheilungen zur vaterländischen Geschichte* XVI (1877), 60-61.)

20. Egli, p. 394, *Varia* 5, lines 7-8.

> Suppeditant festo tria gaudia: pax, pater, esto!
> Fax, lavacrum, vinum trinum testantur et unum.

21. Egli, *Varia* 5, lines 9-11.

22. Egli, *Varia* 5, lines 15-21.

23. Egli, *Varia* 5, lines 22-24.

24. P.Piper, *Die Schriften Notkers und seiner Schule* (Freiburg and Tübingen, 1882) I,112, quotes a passage interpolated by Notker into his translation of Boethius where he describes a globe made recently in the abbey under the direction of Abbot Burchard.

25. Edited by Piper, I,685-848.

26. Egli, p. 396, *Varia* 5, lines 27-30.

27. Egli, *Varia* 5, lines 31-36.

28. Egli, *Varia* 5, lines 38-40.

29. Von Knonau, *Ekkeharti Casus,* cap. 89, p. 317: "Nam cum apud suum Gallum ambas scolas suas teneret, nemo praeter exiles pusiones quicquam alteri, nisi Latine, ausus est proloqui."

30. Egli, p. 230, XLIV, line 62: "Primus barbaricam scribens faciensque saporam."

31. Ibid.: "Teutonice propter caritatem discipulorum plures libros exponens."

32. Piper, I,859-860.

33. The epithet occurs in several places, notably at the end of his translation of the Athanasian Creed. See Piper, II,644:

> Notker Teutonicus domino finitur amicus,
> Gaudeat ille locis in paradysiacis.

34. Piper, I,860-861.

35. E.H.Sehrt and Taylor Starck in their edition of the Martianus Capella translation (*Notkers des Deutschen Werke,* Halle/Saale, 1935) have printed at the foot of each page the corresponding section of Remigius' commentary that Notker used.

36. Piper, I,686–847.

37. Piper, I,1–363.

38. M.Manitius, *Geschichte der lateinischen Literatur des Mittelalters* (Munich, 1911), II, 696; P.T.Hoffmann, *Der mittelaltliche Mensch gesehen aus Welt und Umwelt Notkers des Deutschen* (Gotha, 1922), p. 143.

39. G.Ehrismann, *Geschichte der deutschen Literatur bis zum Ausgang des Mittelalters* (Munich, 1932), I,452–457.

40. Piper, I,861.

41. J.K.Bostock, *A Handbook of Old High German Literature* (Oxford, 1955), p. 256.

42. W.P.Ker, *The Dark Ages* (New York, 1958 reprint), p. 202: "Notker's style is enough to place him among the masters."

43. Clark, *The Abbey,* p. 249.

44. Piper, II,1–606.

45. Piper, I,623–684. The authorship of these tracts has been questioned. See L.M.DeRijk, "On the Curriculum of the Arts of the Trivium at St. Gall from c.850 – c.1000," *Vivarium* I (1963), 51–53.

46. See Piper, I,673–674. The first two illustrate poetic imagery that appeals through the ear, as he quotes four lines on the sounds of battle and four lines on hunting the wild boar. The third illustrates hyperbole as he gives five lines, again on the wild boar.

47. Piper, I, 591–622.

48. Edited from a single manuscript, by P.Piper in *Nachträge zur alteren deutschen National-Literatur* CLXII (1897-98),312–318.

49. Piper, I,851–859.

50. For a treatment of the library and the manuscripts, see Clark, pp. 273–284, and J.W.Thompson, *The Medieval Library* (Chicago, 1939), pp. 195–197.

51. In his letter to Bishop Hugo (Piper, I,860) Notker asks for parchment and for money to pay for copying the manuscripts.

52. G.Scherrer, *Verzeichniss der Handschriften der Stiftsbibliothek von St. Gallen* (Halle, 1875), p. 202, Cod. 621, f. 351: "Utilis multum liber, sed vitio scriptoris mendosus. . . . Plura in hoc libro fatuitate cuiusdam ut sibi videbatur male asscripta. Domnus Notkerus abradi et utiliora iussit in locis asscribi. Assumptis ergo duobus exemplaribus quae deo dante valuimus, tanti viri iudicio fecimus."

53. Scherrer, p. 134, Cod. 393, and Egli, iii.

54. In Cod. 621, above these lines, Ekkehard has written: "Has duas lineas amandas domnus Notkerus scripsit. Vivat anima eius in domino." This is reproduced in *M.G.H. SS.* II,tab.VI.

55. Egli, p. 233, XLIV, lines 81–82:

> Hic finis hominis post imparis eruditoris,
> Pneumate, quem fotum replevit gratia totum.

56. *Vita Fridolini Confessoris Seckingensis auctore Balthero* in *M.G.H. SS. Rerum Merovingicarum* III,354, where his pupil, Baltherus, speaks of his "mitissima correctione."

57. Hoffmann, *Der mittelaltliche Mensch,* p. 143.

58. Egli, pp. 231-234, XLIV, lines 68-83.

59. E. Dümmler and H. Wartmann, *St. Galler Todtenbuch,* p. 45. In the *Annales Sangallenses Maiores* (*M.G.H. SS.* I, 62) for the year 1022, the author records: "Notker, nostrae memoriae hominum doctissimus et benignissimus."

60. Piper, II,644.

61. Ekkehard's life (980-1060) was spent largely at St. Gall except for a few years when he went to teach at the cathedral school at Mainz. See E.Dümmler, "Ekkehard IV von St. Gallen," *Zeitschrift für deutsches Altertum,* XIV (1869), 1-73.

62. In a gloss on the *Liber Benedictionum* XLIV, line 69 (Egli, p. 232) where Ekkehard tells of Notker's devotion to St. Peter, he says, "Mihi quoque dicere solebat: roga, Ekkehart, clavigerum caeli, ut tibi aperiat. Spera in eum et ipse faciet." Notker's *Computus* was dedicated to Ekkehard: "Notger Ekkehardo discipulo de quatuor quaestionibus computi." (Cod. *B.N.* Nouv. acq., 229, f. 252, described by L. Delisle, *Mélanges de Paléographie et de Bibliographie,* Paris, 1880, p. 456.)

63. É.Lesne, *Les Écoles,* V, 413.

64. Von Knonau, *Ekkeharti Casus* cap. 80, pp. 286-289.

65. Von Knonau, *Ekkeharti Casus* caps. 33-46, pp. 126-165. J.V. von Scheffel has made these incidents and characters the basis of his novel, *Ekkehard* (Reprinted, New York, 1940).

66. *Vita Fridolini* (*M.G.H. SS. Rerum Merovingicarum III,* 354).

67. Egli, p. 234, XLIV, line 86.

Notes to Chapter VIII

1. Anselm, *Gesta episcoporum Tungrensium, Traiectensium et Leodiensium* cap. 30 (*M.G.H. SS.* VII, 206).

2. Gozechinus Scholasticus, *Epistola ad Vacherum itidem scholasticum olim discipulum* (*P.L.* CXLIII, 889).

3. S.Balau cites as evidence for this the fact that students from all over Europe sought out the school of Liège. See his "Les sources de l'histoire du pays de Liège au Moyen Age," *Mémoires couronnés et Mémoires de savants étrangers de l'Académie royale de Belgique* LXI (1902-5), 146-151.

4. Given by Gilles d'Orval (Aegidius Aureaevallensis) in his *Gesta episcoporum Leodiensium* (*M.G.H. SS.* XXV, 60).

5. Besides Gilles d'Orval's short account, Anselm (*Gesta,* caps. 25-30) has furnished the only other eleventh-century record of Notger's life. A long account found in a fourteenth-century chronicle of Jean d'Outremeuse (*Ly Myreur des Histoirs* IV, 132-182, ed. A. Bourgnet, Brussels, 1877) is too fanciful to

be reliable. It is interesting, however, that the author stresses the educational activities of the bishop.

6. One contemporary source, the *Annales Hildesheimenses* (*M.G.H. SS.* II, 93) noting his death in 1008, says that he was a provost at St. Gall, but he is not mentioned by historians of St. Gall.

7. G.Kurth in *Notger de Liège et la civilisation au Xe siècle* (Brussels, 1905), p. 257 suggests this possibility.

8. E.de Moreau in his *Histoire de l'Église en Belgique* (Brussels, 1945), II, p. 30, after giving an account of his works concludes, "Tous ces travaux mériteraient déjà à Notger le titre de second fondateur de Liège." See also Kurth, *Notger,* p. 130.

9. The *Vita* in Gilles d'Orval, p. 61, cites this title.

10. On occasion, Notger found himself opposed to the position of Gerbert in Church politics. When, for example, he disagreed with him on the question of the archbishop of Rheims, Gerbert wrote to Notger asking him to reconsider his stand, mentioning his old friendship for the bishop. See H.P.Lattin, *The Letters of Gerbert* (New York, 1961), letter 202, pp.263-4.

11. Anselm, *Gesta* cap. 30, p. 206.

12. *Vita* p. 62.

13. Anselm, *Gesta* cap. 29, p. 205.

14. Anselm, *Gresta* cap 28, p.205.

15. Kurth, *Notger,* p. 267, calls it the "pépinière de clerics."

16. The incident is related in Anselm, *Gesta,* cap. 29, pp. 205-6.

17. Rupert in his *Chronicon S.Laurentii Leodiensis* (*M.G.H. SS.* VIII, 266) describes Leo's sojourn in Liège.

18. Anselm, *Gesta,* cap. 30, p. 206.

19. Anselm, *Gesta,* cap. 40, pp. 210-11.

20. *Gesta abbatum Lobiensium, Continuatio* II (*M.G.H. SS.* XXI, 309).

21. *Adelmanni Scholastici rythmi alphabetici* in M.Bouquet, *Recueil des historiens des Gaules et de la France* (Paris, 1876), XI, 438.

22. Anselm, *Gesta,* cap. 29, pp. 205-206.

23. É.Lesne, *Histoire de la propriété ecclésiastique en France,* vol V *Les Écoles* (Lille, 1940), pp. 354-5.

24. Edited by E.Voigt (Halle,1889). See above, p. 8.

25. Of special pertinence are the verses beginning at 1145: De insipiente magistro et discipulis, and at 1253: De immitibus magistris et pigris.

26. Kurth, *Notger,* p. 284, discusses his studies in geometry.

27. Now in the Musée Curtius at Liège, it is described by J. Philippe, "L'Évangéliare de Notger et la chronologie de l'art mosan dans les époques pré-romane et romane," *Académie royale de Belgique,* Classe des Beaux-arts, Mémoires X (1956) pp. 34-55.

28. De Moreau, *L'Histoire,* II, p. 310, gives a specific date for the scene represented when he says, "Il s'agit donc du fameux évèque Notger qui donna sans doute à l'église St-Jean, en 982, l'évangéliare dont ce feuillet formait une des couvertures."

29. *Ex miraculis s. Adalhardi Corbeiensis, M.G.H. SS.* XV (2), 859.

30. J.Warichez in *L'Abbaye de Lobbes* (Louvain, 1909), p. 68, says, "L'école monastique et la culture des lettres surtout brillent d'un vif éclat. Lobbes devint le centre intellectuel le plus fameux du diocèse de Liège."

31. Folcuin, *Gesta abbatum Lobiensium M.G.H. SS.* IV, cap. 19, p. 63.

32. S.Balau, *Les sources de l'histoire du pays de Liège,* pp. 102-117, gives a comprehensive account of Folcuin's achievements. See also Warichez, pp. 246-256.

33. *Continuatio,* II, *M.G.H. SS.* XXI, 309-310.

34. *Annales Laubienses, M.G.H. SS.* IV, 18 for the year 989.

35. *Gesta episcoporum Cameracensium, M.G.H. SS.* VII, 445-446.

36. Ibid. "Qui et studeat plus amari quam timeri."

37. H.Kurth, in *Biographie nationale de Belgique* IX, 246, concludes his biography of Heriger by saying, "Heriger est certainement un des types les plus remarquables du lettré au Xᵉ siècle."

38. *Continuatio* II, p. 309. Warichez, *Lobbes,* pp. 254-256, gives the list of fifty-two volumes. See J.W.Thompson, *The Medieval Library, p. 220.*

39. In the *Elevatio S.Landoaldi, M.G.H. SS.* XV (2) 610, "Herigerum didascalum ac musicae artis peritum." In Heriger's preface to his *Vita Remacli* (*P.L.* CXXXIX, 1150), he makes reference to the method employed in teaching rhetoric. His writings include subjects in the fields of arithmetic and dialetic.

40. *Gesta abbatum Gemblacensium, M.G.H. SS.* VIII, 536.

41. Ibid., p. 541.

42. *Continuatio* II, p. 310. Of Olbert, Wazo, and Hugo, Warichez, *Lobbes,* p. 69, says, "Les plus grands célébrités littéraires de la Lotharingie, au XIᵉ siècle sortirent de l'école de Lobbes."

43. *Vita Theodorici Andaginesis, M.G.H. SS.* XII, 38-41. For an account of his career, see Warichez, *Lobbes,* pp. 141-148.

44. Biographers of Heriger usually name the two bishops as early pupils of Heriger (e.g. O.Hirzel, "Heriger, Abt von Lobbes," *Beiträge zur Kulturgeschichte des Mittelalters und der Renaissance,* VIII (1910), p. 21), but there is little evidence of any prolonged training at Lobbes.

45. Kurth, *Biog. Nat.* IX, 245 names him "Le plus ancien historiographe de la Belgique."

46. *Gesta episcoporum Tungrensium, Traiectensium, et Leodiensium, M.G.H. SS.* VII, 162-189.

47. Ibid., 189-238.

48. *P.L.* CXXXIX, 1147-1168.

49. Only a fragment of this metrical composition has been preserved. See *P.L.* CXXXIX, 1125-1168.

50. *P.L.* CXXXIX, 1110-1124. This includes the companions of St. Land-oaldus, the so-called "Winterhoven saints."

51. *P.L.* CXXXIX, 1141-48.

52. This is mentioned in *Chronica Alberici monachi Trium Fontium, M.G.H. SS.* XXIII, 775. It is printed with the works of Gerbert, *Gerberti Opera mathematica,* edited by N.Bubnov (Berlin, 1889) pp. 205-225.

53. *P.L.* CXXXIX, 1129-1136.

54. Sigebertus, *De scriptoribus ecclesiasticis,* 137 (*P.L.* CLX, 578).

55. *Continuatio* II, 309.

56. *Dicta Domini Herigeri abbatis de corpore et sanguine Domini, P.L.* CXXXIX, 179-188. He is also credited with another collection, unpublished, entitled *Exaggeratio plurimum auctorum de corpore et sanguine Domini.*

57. *Epistola ad Hugonem* (*P.L.* CXXXIX, 1134).

58. *Continuatio* II, 309.

Notes to Chapter IX

1. Hrotsuitha, *Gesta Oddonis* (*M.G.H. SS.* IV,320).

2. Thietmar, *Chronicon* II,16 (ed. F.Kurze, Hanover, 1889), p. 28.

3. Sigebert, *Vita Deoderici episcopi Mettensis* I.1 (*M.G.H. SS.* IV,464).

4. *Vita Brunonis archiepiscopi Coloniensis* (*M.G.H. SS.*IV,252-275). A *Vita Brunonis altera* was compiled chiefly from Ruotger in the thirteenth century (Ibid., 275-279). All references designated *Vita* will be to Ruotger.

5. *Vita,* cap. 3, p. 255.

6. Radbod had been trained at the Palatine school of Charles the Bald by the scholar, Manno. See Manitius, *Geschichte* I,603.

7. *Vita,* cap. 4, p. 256.

8. *Vita Iohannis abbatis Gorziensis, auctore Iohanne abbate S. Arnulfi,* cap. 116 (*M.G.H. SS.* IV,370).

9. *Vita,* cap. 8, p. 257.

10. Ibid.: "sicuti arcam dominicam."

11. Ibid.

12. Widukind (*Res gestae Saxonicae,* II.36, *M.G.H. SS.* III,448) testifies "prudentissimus erat consultor."

13. *Vita,* cap. 5, p. 256.

14. Ibid.

15. *Vita,* cap. 8, p. 257 and cap. 33, p. 267. Excerpts from some of his speeches are given in proof of his eloquence.

16. *Vita,* cap. 7, p. 257.

17. Folcuin, *Gesta abbatum Lobiensium,* cap. 22 (*M.G.H. SS.* IV,64).

18. *Gesta Ottonis.* (*M.G.H. SS.* III, 340-346).

19. *Vita,* cap. 5, p. 256.

20. *Vita Mahthildis reginae,* cap. 9 (*M.G.H. SS.* IV,289).

21. Ibid.

22. *Vita,* cap. 11, p. 258.

23. Kurth, *Notger* p. 2.
24. *Vita,* cap. 49, p. 295: "Bruno pacificus."
25. *Vita,* cap. 41, p. 270.
26. *Vita,* cap. 1, p. 254.
27. Sigebert, *Vita Deoderici* I.2, p. 464.
28. *Vita,* cap. 48, p. 274.
29. *Vita Deoderici,* I.7, p. 467

Notes to Chapter X

1. *Vita sancti Wolfgangi episcopi Ratisbonensis, auctore Othlone monacho* cap. 7 (*M.G.H. SS.* IV, 528.)

2. *Vita,* cap. 1, p. 527. All references are to Othlo's *Life.*

3. Arnold, *Liber de miraculis beati Emmerammi,* cap. 2 (*M.G.H. SS* IV, 556), "genere nobilissimus."

4. *Vita,* cap. 2, p. 527. The biographer points out two parallels for the use of the word "wolf," as it is applied in a complimentary sense to Benjamin, son of Jacob (*Gen.* 49.27) and to St. Paul by an unnamed poet in the verse: "O lupe Paule rapax."

5. The *Vita* was written about 1052 at the urgent request of the monks of St. Emmeram.

6. *Liber de miraculis* (*M.G.H. SS.* IV, 521-541.) Another early biography, written anonymously, has been lost.

7. *Vita,* cap. 7, p. 529: "Et nutricis more quasi lacteum historiae cibum praecoquens suppeditaret."

8. *Vita,* cap. 10, p. 529: "At ille domum veniens, ab omnibus cognatis et amicis amabiliter est susceptus, obviamque habuit, ut ita dicam, Syrenes velut alter Ulyxes."

9. *Vita,* cap. 10, p. 530. Gregory served as abbot from 960 to 996. He is said to have been the son of King Edward of England. See *Acta Sanctorum* LXVI, p. 571.

10. *Vita,* cap. 10, p. 530.

11. *Vita,* cap. 14, p. 531.

12. J.W.Thompson, *The Medieval Library,* p. 201.

13. *Vita,* cap. 18, pp. 534-5.

14. *Vita,* cap. 28, p. 538, "impeditioris linguae erat." Yet again the biographer speaks of his "melliti oris dulcedinem." (*Vita,* cap. 19, p. 535.)

15. *Vita,* cap. 19, p. 535.

16. The biographer devotes a large part of his sketch to the miracles

performed both during his lifetime and after his death. St. Wolfgang was canonized by Pope Leo IX in 1052.

17. *Vita*, cap. 28, pp. 537-8. This is reminiscent of the famous debate between Gerbert and Othric before Otto.

18. *Vita*, cap. 30, p. 538.

19. *Vita*, cap. 42, p. 542.

20. Thietmar, *Chronicon*, V,praef. (*M.G.H. SS*. III, 107).

21. Thietmar, *Chronicon* V, cap. 42 (*M.G.H. SS*. III, 130).

22. *Gesta Trevorum*, *M.G.H. SS*. VIII, 175.

23. *Acta sanctorum* LXVI. 1. 549-550.

24. For the representation of this episode, see K.Künstle, *Ikonographie der Heiligen* (Freiburg,1926) II,596-601, and L.Réau *Iconographie de l'art chrétienne* (Paris,1959), 1348-50.

25. *Acta sanctorum*, p. 550.

Notes to Chapter XI

1. "Qui patriae stemma radians ut gemma serena." The line comes from Bernward's epitaph, as given by Thangmar, *Vita Bernwardi episcopi*, cap. 59 (*M.G.H. SS*. IV, p. 782). This biography is the main source for Bernward's life and all references, under *Vita*, will be to it.

2. *Vita*, cap. 2, p. 759.

3. The reliquary is described by F.J.Tschan, *Saint Bernward of Hildesheim* (Notre Dame, 1942-1952), II, 85-95, and III, plates 82-88.

4. Tschan (I, 1-6) discusses fully the background of Bernward.

5. *Vita*, cap. 1, p. 758.

6. *Translatio S. Epiphanii*, cap. 2 (*M.G.H. SS*. IV, 249). The large collection of books that Othwin brought from Italy formed the nucleus of the cathedral library.

7. *Vita*, cap. 1, p. 758.

8. Tschan (I, 18) cites two notable occasions when Bernward was called upon for his medical knowledge.

9. *Vita*, cap. 1, p. 758.

10. *Vita*, cap. 2, p. 759.

11. Ibid.

12. Ibid. See above, note 2.

13. *Vita*, cap. 4, p. 759; *Annales Hildesheimenses*, Anno 993. (*M.G.H. SS*. III, 69).

14. Tschan, I, 1.

15. *Vita*, cap. 19, p. 767. A year later, Bernward and Thangmar attended Otto's funeral at Aachen. See *Vita* cap. 34, p. 773.

16. *Vita,* cap. 53, p. 780.

17. *Vita,* cap. 5, pp. 759-760.

18. *Vita,* cap. 8, p. 762.

19. *Vita,* cap. 6, p. 760.

20. *Vita,* cap. 1, p. 758.

21. *Annales Hildesheimenses,* Anno 1013. (*M.G.H. SS.* III, 94).

22. In recording the disaster, the annalist particularly mourns the loss of so many irreplaceable manuscripts.

23. Tschan, II, 1-70; III, plates 1-78.

24. Tschan, II, 36-37; III, plates 57-58.

25. Tschan, II, 54; III, plate 78.

26. R.Lloyd, *The Golden Middle Age* (London, 1937) p. 27.

27. F.J.Tschan, "Bernward of Hildesheim," in *Mediaeval and Historiographical Essays for J.W.Thompson,* edited by J.L.Cate and E.N.Andrews (Chicago, 1938), pp. 339-340, speaks of the "educational objective" of these works.

28. *Vita,* cap. 6, p. 760.

29. Ibid.

30. This is described in Tschan, *St. Bernward,* II, 271-350, and illustrated in III, plates 147-191.

31. They are described in Tschan, II, 141-270, and illustrated in III, plates 115-136.

32. *Vita,* cap. 8, p. 762.

33. *Vita,* cap. 46, p. 778.

34. Jacobus da Voragine in his *Golden Legend* for the feast of St. Michael on September 29 records the many appearances of the saint in early medieval times.

35. *Narratio de canon, et transl. S.Bernwardi,* cap. 1-13, G.W.F. von Leibnitz, *Scriptores rerum Brunsvicensium* I, (Hanover, 1707) 469-476.

36. They are described by Tschan, II, 129-140, III; plates 107-114.

37. *Vita,* cap. 57, p. 784.

Notes to Chapter XII

1. Letter 196, written in 995 to his old teacher, Raymond. All references to and translations from the letters will be to the edition of H.P.Lattin, *The Letters of Gerbert* (N.Y., 1961).

2. Richer, *Historiarum libri IV,* III, 43, edition and French translation of R.Latouche (Paris, 1930-1937), II, 50-2. Richer, a monk of Rheims, a devoted student of Gerbert, is the chief contemporary source for the life of Gerbert.

3. An evaluation of the abbey is given by A.Olleris in "Gerbert, Aurillac et son monastère," *Mémoires de l'Académie des sciences, belles-lettres et art de Clermont-Ferrand* (1862), B IV, 161-190.

4. Presumably he studied at the monastery of Santa Maria de Ripoll. Lattin, *Letters,* p.3.

5. Abbot Guarin is mentioned in two of Gerbert's letters, Letter 25, where he speaks of a book on arithmetic that Guarin left at Aurillac, and Letter 51, where he recalls Guarin's encouragement during difficult times.

6. In Letter 32, Gerbert requests a book on astronomy that Lobet had translated, presumably from the Arabic. See H.P.Lattin, "Lupitus Barchinonensis," *Speculum* VII (1932), 58-64.

7. In Letter 33, Gerbert asks Bishop Bonfill for the book *De multiplicatione et divisione numerorum* of Joseph the Wise.

8. Richer, *Historiae* III,44.

9. Ibid.

10. Gerbert himself points out in Letter 171 that his enemies, specifically Duke Charles, were responsible for this title. The two kings were Hugh Capet and Otto III.

11. Besides Richer, Thietmar, bishop of Merseburg (976-1018), says of him, "Optime callebat astrorum cursus discernere et contemporales suos variae artis noticia superare." *Chronicon* VII,40 (ed. Kurze, p. 191). Helgaud, monk at Fleury, abbot in 1004, and finally archbishop of Bourges, says, "Is quippe Girbertus, pro maxime suae sapientiae merito, qua toto radiabat in mundo," *Helgaldi sive Helgaudi Epitoma vitae Roberti regis, P.L.* CXLI, 911.

12. H.O.Taylor, *The Mediaeval Mind* (London, 1938) I,286.

13. O.G.Darlington, "Gerbert, the Teacher," *American Historical Review* LII (1947) 456-7.

14. Richer, *Historiae,* III,45.

15. In one of his letters (16) he sends a request for Demosthenes Philalethes' *Ophthalmicus.* In two other letters (122 and 159), he refers to requests for his medical assistance, but he says he has always avoided the practice of medicine. Richer, his pupil, became a keen student of the science, as he attests in his *Historiae* (IV, 50).

16. Letter 201, where he quotes the *Aeneid* I,3.

17. In a letter from Otto III (230), the emperor speaks of Gerbert's "scientiae flamma."

18. In Letter 175 to Abbot Romulf who had sent him some of the works of Cicero, he says, "Continue as you have begun and offer the waters of Cicero to one who thirsts." In Letters 51 and 105 he speaks of the "fruits" of the liberal disciplines.

19. Richer, *Historiae,* III,55.

20. Letter 50.

21. Richer, *Historiae,* III,42-43.

22. F.M.Carey, "The Scriptorium of Rheims during the Archbishopric of Hincmar (845-882 A.D.)," *Studies in Honor of E.K.Rand* (N.Y., 1938), 41-60.

23. Letter 50.

24. Numerous references to this book-collecting activity are found in Letters, 14,15,16,25,32,33,50,92,124,132,138,142,156,158.

25. Richer, *Historiae,* III,46.

26. An important study of two eleventh-century manuscripts by H.P.Lattin reveals in one a list of treatises on dialectic available to Gerbert, and in another the text of many of these works. ("The Eleventh-Century MS Munich 14436," *Isis* XXXVIII 1947-8, 222-225.).

27. Richer, *Historiae,* III,55-65.

28. *P.L.* CXXXIX, 179-188. This is an elaboration of the question raised by Boethius in his *Dialogus II in Porphyrium (P.L.* LXIV,57).

29. Richer, *Historiae* III,47.

30. Letter 175.

31. See R.Latouche, "Un imitateur de Salluste au Xe siècle, l'historien Richer," *Annales de l'Université de Grenoble,*Nouv. serie, Section Lettres-Droit VI (1929) 289-305.

32. See above, chapter II.

33. Syrus, *Vita Sancti Maioli (P.L.*CXXXVII,755).

34. *Leonis Abbatis et Legati ad Hugonem et Robertum reges Epistola (M.G.H. SS* III,687).

35. Letter 138.

36. Letter 92.

37. Letter 105.

38. Richer, *Historiae* III,48.

39. In Letter 50, Gerbert discusses the honorable and the useful and concludes that for people in public life there is no way of separating speaking well from living well.

40. Letter 74.

41. Among the contemporary sources, only Adémar de Chabannes (*Chronicon* III,31, *P.L.* CXLI,49) states that he went to Cordova. See Darlington, "Gerbert," 460-463.

42. Letter 3.

43. Letter 230. H.P.Lattin (*Letters,* p.295, note 2) suggests that the manuscript may have been MS. Bamberg, Class 5 (HJ.IV.12) written on purple parchment in gold letters originally made for Charles the Bald soon after 832.

44. For a discussion of Gerbert's part in the transmission of the Arabic numbers, see H.P.Lattin, "The origin of our present system of notation," *Isis* XIX (1933),181-194.

45. Richer, *Historiae,* III,54.

46. M.Chasles, "Explication des traités de l'abacus," *Histoire de l'Arithmétique* (Paris, 1843), 1-27.

47. Letter 7.

48. N.M.Bubnov, *Gerberti opera mathematica* (Berlin, 1899), 8-22.

49. A.Olleris,*Oeuvres de Gerbert* (Clermont-Ferrand and Paris, 1867, 357-422), gives the text of the *Liber abaci* of Bernelinus who says (357) that it was invented by Gerbert.

50. Ibid., xxxvii and 593. Gerbert himself was so impressed by the abacus that he used it twice in two fine metaphors. At the end of a letter to Otto III, he says, "May the last number of the abacus be the length of your life." (Letter 227). Legend has it that when he was *in extremis,* Gerbert said, "Nil abacus mathesisque tibi, Giberte, iuvabant." (*Chronicon* of St. Andrew of Cambrai, *M.G.H. SS* VII,527).

51. Letter 233. See Lattin, *Letters,* pp. 301-302, note 2.

52. Olleris, *Oeuvres,* 401-470; Bubnov, *Opera,* 48-97.

53. J.Leflon, *Gerbert* (Paris, 1946), pp. 87-88.

54. See M. Destombes, "Un astrolabe carolingien et l'origine de nos chiffres arabes," *Archives internationales d'histoire des sciences,* XV, no. 58-59 (1962), pp. 3-45. H. Gunther in his *Astrolabes of the World* (Oxford, 1932), p. 230, no. 101, Plate III, presents an astrolabe now in Florence (Galileo Tribuna) known as the astrolabe of Pope Sylvester II. H.P.Lattin, who expressed doubt concerning the attribution of the *Liber de astrolabio* to Gerbert (*Letters,* pp. 6 and 47, note 11), assures me that she now considers the work genuine.

55. St. Andrew of Cambrai, *Loc. cit.,* says, "Geometria quoque adeo peritus, ut spatia locorum vel in terra vel in aere solo intuitu facile metiretur."

56. Richer, *Historiae* III,49. "Multo ante Galliis ignotam notissimam effecit."

57. Ibid.

58. Letter 105. Lattin (*Letters,* p. 141, n. 5) suggests that a new technique, finger-action, (as opposed to the old hand-technique) for playing the organ that developed at this time may have originated with Gerbert.

59. Letter 77.

60. Letter 77 to Abbot Gerald of Aurillac, Letter 102 to Raymond of Aurillac, and Letter 171 also to Raymond.

61. Letters 4 and 5.

62. In Letter 32 to Lobet of Barcelona he asks the recipient to send him the book *De astrologia* translated by himself, probably from the Arabic.

63. Letter 15, where he calls it *De astrologia.*

64. Letter 138, where it is called "M.Manlius *De astrologia.*"

65. Letter 161.

66. Richer, *Historiae* III,50. Lattin, *Astronomy* "Symposium on the Tenth Century, *Mediaevalia et Humanistica* IX (1955), p. 15, discusses this.

67. In Letter 156, Gerbert wrote to Remi of Trier (in 989) that he had begun work on such a sphere, a difficult piece of work, which, if properly marked in colors, would take a year to complete. See also Letters, 142, 160, and 170.

68. Richer, *Historiae,* III,52. Lattin, *Astronomy,* p. 16.

69. Apparently Gerbert did not adopt the theory of Martianus Capella who taught that the orbits of Mercury and Venus are around the sun.

70. Richer, *Historiae,* III,50.

71. Richer, *Historiae,* III,50. Lattin, *Astronomy,* 14.

72. Letter 2. See E.Zinner, "Gerbert und das Sehrohr," *Bericht der Natur-forschungen Gesellschaft Bamberg,* XXXII (1952), 39-40. For illustrations of this

device, see H.Michel, "Les tubes optiques avant le télescope," *Ciel et Terre* LXX (1954),175-184.

73. Letter 2.

74. Richer, *Historiae,* III,51.

75. Richer, *Historiae,* III,53. Lattin, *Astronomy,* 15.

76. Richer, *Historiae,* III,53.

77. Letter 51.

78. Letter 52.

79. Letters 43,77.

80. Letter 102.

81. Ibid.

82. Letter 196.

83. Letter 105.

84. Ibid. Of Constantine, he says, "He is very closely joined to me in friendship."

85. Letter 92.

86. Letter 6.

87. Letter 7.

88. Letters 142, 156, 160, 170.

89. Richer, *Historiae,* IV,50.

90. Richer, *Historiae,* III,55.

91. Darlington, "Gerbert," 473.

92. Helgaldus, *Epitoma vitae Rotberti regis* (*P.L.* CXLI,911).

93. Richer (*Historiae* III,85) speaks of a conference between Hugh and Otto II when Hugh took an interpreter so that he might translate Otto's Latin.

94. Richer, *Historiae* IV,13. See C.Pfister, *Études sur la règne de Robert le Pieux* (Paris, 1885), pp. 34-40.

95. Letter 230.

96. Letter 232.

97. Letter 231.

98. Letter 226.

99. Olleris, *Oeuvres* clxviii, and H.K.Mann, *The Lives of the Popes in the early Middle Ages* (London, 1925) V, 63.

100. H.Bloch, "Beiträge zur Gerschichte des Bischofs Leon von Vercelli und seiner Zeit," *Neues Archiv* XXII (1897), 115.

101. "Adalberonis episcopi Laudunensis Carmen ad Robertum regem," in M.Bouquet, *Recueil des Historiens des Gaules et de la France* (Paris, 1760), X,67.

102. Picavet, *Gerbert: un pape philosophe* (Paris, 1897), p. 21.

103. Willelmi Malmesbirensis Monachi *Gesta regum Anglorum* II,167-173, ed. T.D.Hardy (London, 1840) pp. 271-284. Besides William, the chief writers are Sigebert of Gembloux, Odericus Vitalis, and Vincent of Beauvais.

104. An anonymous epigram, purporting to be the words of Gerbert, but written centuries later, reads; "Do not be surprised that ignorant people incapable of knowing the truth think that I am a magician; I studied that science of Archimedes and philosophy at a time when it was a great glory to know nothing." See Bouquet, *Recueil,* X,260.

105. This is seen in references in his letters, but it is emphasized in Letter 192, which is a profession of faith upon his elevation to the archbishopric of Rheims.

106. A modern biography of Gerbert is entitled: *Gerbert; Humanisme et Chrétienté au Xe siècle,* by J.Leflon (Paris, 1946).

107. Picavet, *Gerbert,* pp. 118-119.

108. They are: *Geometria; Liber abaci; Regula de abaco computi; Libellus de numerorum divisione; Libellus de rationali et ratione uti.* The authenticity of a theological treatise *Libellus de corpore et sanguine Domini* (*P.L.* CXXXIX, 179-188) has been questioned.

109. Letter 175.

110. Letter 51.

111. Letter 132.

112. Leflon, *Gerbert,* 74, says, "Boëce fut évidemment le livre de chevet du maître rémois et il en est tellement mourri que, non seulement pour exalter sa science, mais encore pour caractériser sa manière, la *Chronique de Verdun* l'appellé 'un second Boëce.'"

113. *P.L.* CXXXIX,287.

114. Olleris, *Oeuvres,* 471.

Notes to Chapter XIII

1. Daniel XII,3. Everaclus' biographer uses this as a kind of requiem for the great master. Reinerus, *Vita Everacli, M.G.H. SS.* XX, 565.

2. Second preface to the plays, *Opera,* ed. K.Strecker (Leipzig, 1906), p. 115; English translation of E.S.Duckett, *Life and Death,* p. 260.

3. *Hymnus de Sancto Dunstano Episcopo,* Stubbs, *Memorials,* p. 441.

4. *Liber Eliensis,* ed. D.J.Stewart, II, p. 105.

5. *Historia Rameseiensis,* ed. W.D.Macray, I, p. 28.

6. *Vita Abbonis, P.L.* CXXXIX, 393.

7. Ruotger, *Vita Brunonis, M.G.H. SS.* IV, cap. 49, p. 275.

8. *Helgaldi sive Helgaudi Epitoma vite Roberti regis, P.L.* CXLI, 911.

9. Dame Grammar is depicted in a number of the manuscripts of Martianus Capella, as, for example, *Bibliothèque Nationale* lat. 7900A, f. 127v.

10. *Praeloquia, P.L.* CXXXVI, 176: "Opta magis amari, quam timeri." He also says that the teacher should so conduct his class that he quicken the minds of his pupils rather than deaden them.

11. *Fecunda ratis,* ed. E.Voigt, p. 2.

12. Aegidius, *Gesta episcoporum Leodiensium, M.G.H. SS.* XXV, p. 62.

13. *Praeloquia,* 175.

14. First preface to the plays, *Opera*, pp. 113-114.

15. J.Dubois-Olivier, *Vetus Bibliotheca*, p. 302.

16. This inscription, in Greek, appears over the door of the library of St. Gall which houses the remains of the books of the old abbey library.

17. Letter 175. Abbo, too, speaks of the need for the therapy of the library, as he says, "As the hart desireth the water-brooks, so has my soul, trained in the elements of the classic disciplines, longed for the work-filled leisure of philosophic meditation, leisure which I would use for the good of many." (*Apologeticus, P.L.* CXXXIX, 461).

18. Remigius' treatment of *sapientia* in the Martianus commentary is discussed in C.E.Lutz, "Remigius' Ideas on the Classification of the Seven Liberal Arts," *Traditio* XII (1956), pp. 79-80.

19. In addition to references in his own works, testimony to Fulbert's emphasis upon theology is provided in several of the works of his successors. Adelmann, for example, in a poem on Fulbert and his disciples, says, "Tu divina, tu humana excolebas dogmata." (*P.L.* CLXIII, 1295). Angelran of St. Riquier records Fulbert's gift "totius prudentiae, divinae scilicet et humanae." (*P.L.* CLXI, 1423).

20. The Advent antiphons occur in several of the Continental antiphonaries of the ninth and tenth centuries. They seem to have been especially appealing to the English, if one may judge by Cynewulf's poem *Christ*, the first section of which is based upon the "O" antiphons. Although the opening lines and consequently the paraphrase of the O *Sapientia*, are missing, Cynewolf refers to that first antiphon in lines 239-240: "Thou art that Wisdom who with the Lord didst frame all this broad creation."

Selected Bibliography

Included in the list of primary sources are editions of the works of the schoolmasters, contemporary or slightly later accounts of their lives, and early historical records that reveal their influence upon their society. The list of secondary sources includes only those works which have special relevance for an understanding of the masters' lives, their scholarly activities and contributions to learning, and their impact upon their contemporaries.

Primary Sources

Abbo of Fleury. *Opera. P.L.* CXXXIX, 375-562.

Adémar de Chabannes. *Chronicon,* ed. J. Chavanon. Paris, 1897.

Aelfric's Colloquy, ed. G.N.Garmonsway. London, 1947.

Aelfric's De Temporibus Anni, ed. H.Henel. Oxford, 1942. *E.E.T.S.*

Aelfrics Grammatik und Glossar, ed. J.Zupitza. Berlin, 1880.

Aelfric's Lives of the Saints, ed. W.W.Skeat. London, 1881. *E.E.T.S.*

"Aelfric's Version of Alcuini Interrogationes Sigeuulfi in Genesin," ed. G.E.MacLean, *Anglia* VI (1883),425-73; VII (1884), 1-59.

Aimoin. *Historia Francorum. P.L.* CXXXIX, 627-798.

—— *Vita sancti Abbonis. P.L.* CXXXIX, 375-414.

Ancient Laws and Institutes of England, ed. B.Thorpe. London, 1840.

The Anglo-Saxon Version of the Hexameron of St. Basil and Saxon Remains of St. Basil's Admonitio ad Filium Spiritualem, ed. H.W.Norman. London, 1849.

Annales Einsidlenses. M.G.H. SS. III, 137-149.

Annales Hildesheimenses. M.G.H. SS. III, 18-116.

Annales Laubienses. M.G.H. SS. IV,8-28.

Annales Ordinis Sancti Benedicti, ed. J.Mabillon. Lucae, 1739.

*Annales Sangallenses majores. M.G.H. SS.*I,61-82.

Anselm. *Gesta episcoporum Leodiensium. M.G.H. SS.* VII, 189-234.

Arnold. *Liber de miraculis beati Emmerami. M.G.H. SS.* IV,543-74.

Bibliotheca Cluniacensis, ed. M.Marrier, annoted by A.Duchesne. Brussels, 1915, reprint of 1614 edition.

Byrhtferth. *Manual,* ed. S.J.Crawford. London, 1929. *E.E.T.S.*

—— *Opera. P.L.*XC, 188-702.

Chronicon Abbatiae Rameseiensis, ed. W.D.Macray. London, 1886. *R.S.*

Chronicon Monasterii de Abingdon, ed. J. Stevenson. London, 1858. *R.S.*

Ekkehard IV. *Casuum sancti Galli Continuatio,* ed. I.von Arx. *M.G.H. SS.*II, 77-157.

—— ed. G.Meyer von Knonau, *Mittheilungen zur vaterländischen Geschichte* XV-XVI (1877), 1-450.

Floriacensis vetus Bibliotheca, ed. J.DuBois-Olivier. Fleury, 1605.

Folcuin, *Gesta abbatum Lobiensium. M.G. H. SS.*IV,52-74.

Formelbuch des Bischofs Salomo III von Konstanz, ed. E.Dümmler. Leipzig, 1857.

Gerbert. *Opera. P.L.*CXXXIX,85-350.

Gerberti opera mathematica, ed. N.M.Bubnov. Berlin, 1899.

Gesta abbatum Lobbiensium Continuatio. M.G.H. SS. XXI,307-333.

Gilles d'Orval (Aegidius Aureaevallensis). *Gesta episcoporum Leodiensium M.G.H. SS.*XIV,1-135.

Helgaud. *Epitoma vitae Roberti regis. P.L.*CXLI, 909-936.

Heriger. *Gesta episcoporum Tungrensium, Traiectensium et Leodiensium. M.G.H. SS.* VII,131-238.

Heriger. *Opera. P.L.* CXXXIX, 957-1124.

Historians of the Church of York and its Archbishops, ed. J.Raine. London, 1879. *R.S.*

Homilies of the Anglo-Saxon Church: Sermones catholici or Homilies of Aelfric, ed. B.Thorpe. London, 1844-46.

Homilies of Aelfric: A Supplementary Collection, ed. J. Pope. London, 1967. *E.E.T.S.*

John, abbot of St. Arnulfus. *Vita Iohannis abbatis Gorziensis. M.G.H. SS.*IV,335-377.

John of Glastonbury. *Chronicon,* ed. J. Hearne. Oxford, 1726.

John of Salerno. *Vita Odonis. P.L.*CXXXIII,43-86.

The Letters of Gerbert: with his papal privileges as Sylvester II, ed. and tr. H.P.Lattin. New York, 1961.

Lettres de Gerbert (983-987), ed. J.Havet. Paris, 1889.

"Der *Liber Benedictionum* Ekkeharts IV", ed. J.Egli, *Mittheilungen zur vaterländischen Geschichte* XXXI (1909), 1-139.

Liber Eliensis, ed. D.J.Stewart. London, 1848.

Memorials of St. Dunstan, ed. W.Stubbs. London, 1874. *R.S.*

Memorials of St. Edmund's Abbey, ed. T.Arnold. London, 1890. *R.S.*

Monasticon Anglicanum, ed. W.Dugdale. London, 1655.

Narratio de canon. et trans. s. Bernwardi, ed. G.W.F.von Leibnitz, *Scriptores rerum Brunsvicensium* I,469-476. Hanover, 1707.

Notkers des Deutschen Werke, ed. E.H.Sehrt and Taylor Starck. Halle/ Saale, 1935.

Notkers Schriften und seine Schule, ed. P.Piper. Freiburg and Tübingen, 1862.

Odo of Cluny. *Opera. P.L.*CXXXIII, 105-816.

Odonis Abbatis Cluniacensis Occupatio, ed. A. Swoboda. Leipzig, 1900.

Oeuvres de Gerbert, pape sous le nom de Sylvestre II, ed. A.Olleris. Clermont-Ferrand, 1867.

"Les Oeuvres inédites d'Abbon de Fleury," ed. A.Van de Vyver, *Revue Bénédictine* XLVII (1935), 125-169.

Old English Homilies, ed. T.Morris. London, 1848. *E.E.T.S.*

The Old English Version of the Heptateuch, ed. S.J.Crawford. London, 1922. *E.E.T.S.*

"Opuscules mathématiques de Gerbert et de Hériger de Lobbes," ed. H. Omont, *Notices et Extraits* XXXIX (1897), 4-15.

Ordericus Vitalis. *Historia ecclesiastica,* ed. A.Delisle. Paris, 1838.

—— tr. M.Chibnall. Oxford, 1969.

Othlo. *Vita sancti Wolfkangi episcopi Ratisboniensis. M.G.H. SS.* IV, 521-542.

Recueil des Historiens des Gaules et de la France, ed. M. Bouquet. Paris, 1760.

Regularis Concordia, ed. T.Symons. New York, 1953.

Reinerus. *Vita Everacli episcopi Leodiensis M.G.H. SS.*XX, 561-565.

Richer. *Historiarum libri IV,* ed. and tr. R.Latouche. Paris, 1930-1937.

Rodulfus Glaber. *Historiarum libri V,* ed. and tr. M.Prou. Paris, 1886.

Ruotger. *Vita Brunonis archiepiscopi Coloniensis. M.G.H. SS.* IV, 152-279.

Rupert. *Chronicon sancti Laurentii Leodiensis. M.G.H. SS.* VIII,261-279.

St. Odo of Cluny, tr. G. Sitwell. London, 1958.

Sigebert of Gembloux. *Chronicon. P.L.*CLX,57-240.

—— *De scriptoribus ecclesiasticis. P.L.*CLX, 547-593.

—— *Vita Theodorici episcopi Mettensis. M.G.H. SS.* IV,461-483.

Thangmar. *Vita sancti Bernwardi episcopi Hildesheimensis. M.G.H. SS.* IV, 754-782.

Thietmar of Merseburg. *Chronicon,* ed. F. Kurze. Hanover, 1889.

*Vita Mahthildis reginae. M.G.H. SS.*IV,282-302.

Widukind. *Res gestae Saxonicae. M.G.H. SS.* III, 408-467.

William of Malmesbury. *Gesta pontificum Anglorum,* ed. N.E.S.A. Hamilton. London, 1870. *R.S.*

—— *Gesta regum Anglorum,* ed. T.D.Hardy. London, 1840.

Wulfstan. *Vita sancti Aethelwoldi. P.L.* CXXXVII, 79-108.

SECONDARY SOURCES

Allen, Roland. "Gerbert, Pope Silvester II," *English Historical Review* VII (1892), 628-661.

Balau, Sylvain. "Étude critique des sources de l'histoire du pays de Liège au Moyen Age," *Mémoires couronnés et Mémoires de savants étrangers de l'Académie de Belgique* LXI (1902-5), 1-753.

Berlière, Ursmer. "L'Abbaye de Lobbes," *Le Messager des Fidèles* V (1888), 302-99.

Borgmeyer, F. *Die Bernwardische Kunst.* Hildesheim, 1957.

Bostock, J. Knight. *A Handbook of Old High German Literature.* Oxford, 1955.

Cambridge Medieval History III (1922); IV (1966).

Chenesseau, Georges. *L'Abbaye de Fleury à Saint-Benoît-sur-Loire.* Paris, 1931.

Clark, James M. *The Abbey of St. Gall as a Centre of Literature and Art.* Cambridge, 1926.

Cousin, Patrice. *Abbon de Fleury-sur-Loire.* Paris, 1954.

Cuissard-Gaucheron, Charles. *L'École de Fleury-sur-Loire à la fin du Xe siècle et son influence.* Orleans, 1875.

Darlington, Oscar G. "Gerbert, the Teacher," *American Historical Review* LII (1947), 456-476.

Dawson, Christopher. *Religion and the Rise of Western Culture.* Gifford Lectures 1948-49. New York, 1950.

Dubois, Marguerite-Marie. *Aelfric: Sermonnaire, Docteur et Grammairien.* Paris, 1943.

Duckett, Eleanor S. *Death and Life in the Tenth Century.* Ann Arbor, 1967.

—— *Saint Dunstan of Canterbury.* New York, 1955.

Dümmler, Ernst. "Ekkehard IV von St. Gallen," *Zeitschrift für deutsches Altertum* XIV (1869), 1-73.

Ehrismann, Gustav. *Geschichte der deutschen Literatur bis zum Ausgang des Mittelalters*. Munich, 1932-35.

Focillon, Henri. *L'An Mil*. Paris, 1952.

Gallagher, John J. *Church and State in Germany under Otto the Great (963-973)*. Washington D.C., 1938.

Gem, S.H. *An Anglo-Saxon Abbot: Aelfric of Eynsham*. Edinburgh, 1912.

Ghellinck, Joseph de. *Histoire de la littérature latine au Moyen Age*. Paris, 1939.

Hirzel, Oskar. "Heriger, Abt von Lobbes, *"Beiträge zur Kulturgeschichte des Mittelalters und der Renaissance VIII* (1910).

Hoffmann, Paul T. *Der mittelalterliche Mensch gesehen aus Welt und Umwelt Notkers des Deutschen*. Gotha, 1922.

Hunt, Richard W. *Saint Dunstan's Classbook from Glastonbury*. Amsterdam, 1961.

Hurt, James. *Aelfric*. New York, 1972.

Johnson, Edgar N. "The Secular Activities of the German Episcopate, 919-1024," *University of Nebraska Studies* XXX-XXXI (1930-31).

Keller, Hagen. *Kloster Einsiedeln in Ottonischen Schwaben*. Freiburg, 1924.

Ker, W.P. *The Dark Ages*. Reprint New York, 1958.

Knowles, David. *The Monastic Order in England*. Cambridge, 1950.

_____ *The Relig ous Houses of Medieval England*. London, 1940.

Kögel, Rudolf. *Geschichte der deutschen Literatur bis zum Ausgang des Mittelalters*. Strassburg, 1897.

Kolmer, L. *Odo, der erste Cluniacenser Magister*. Deggendorf, 1913.

Krüger, Emil. *Bruns I, Erzbischofs von Köln*. Leipzig, 1876.

Kurth, Godefroid. *Notger de Liège et la civilisation au Xe siècle*. Brussels, 1905.

La Salle de Rochemaure, Duc de. *Gerbert Silvestre II: Le savant, le "faiseur de rois," le pontife*. Paris, 1914.

Lattin, Harriet P. *The Peasant Boy Who Became Pope: Story of Gerbert*. New York, 1961.

Leach, Arthur F. *The Schools of Medieval England*. London, 1916.

Leclercq, Jean. "L'humanisme bénédictin du VIIe au XIIe siècle," *Studia Anselmiana* XX(1948), 1-20.

Lefton, Jean. *Gerbert:Humanisme et chrétienté au Xe siècle*. St. Wandrille, 1916.

Lesne, Émile. *Histoire de la propriété ecclésiastique en France*. Tome V *Les Écoles*. Lille, 1940.

Lloyd, Roger R. *The Golden Middle Age*. London, 1939.

Lopez, Robert S. *The Birth of Europe*. New York, 1967.

——— "Still another Renaissance?" *American Historical Review* LVII (1951-52), 1-11.

——— *The Tenth Century. How Dark the Dark Ages?* New York, 1959.

Lot, Ferdinand. *Les derniers Carolingiens*. Paris, 1891.

——— *Études sur le règne de Hugues Capet et la fin du Xe siècle* Paris, 1903.

——— *Naissance de la France*. Paris, 1948.

Maître, Léon. *Les Écoles épiscopales et monastiques en Occident avant les Universités*. Paris, 1924.

Manitius, Max. *Geschiechte der lateinischen Literatur des Mittelalters*. Munich, 1911-31.

Mann, Horace K. *The Lives of the Popes in the early Middle Ages*. Vol. V. London, 1925.

Mehler, J.B. *Der Heilige Wolfgang, Bischof von Regensburg*. Historische Festschrift. Ratisbon, 1894.

Meier, Gabriel. "Geschichte der Schule von St. Gallen im Mittelalter," *Jahrbuch für Schweitzerische Geschichte* X (1885).

Moreau, Édouard de. *Histoire de l'Eglise en Belgique*. Brussels, 1945.

Olleris, Alexandre, "Gerbert, Aurillac et son monastère," *Mémoires de l'Académie des sciences, belles-lettres et art de Clermont-Ferrand*. Clermont-Ferrand, 1862.

Pardiac, Jean B. *Histoire de Saint Abbon, Abbé de Fleury-sur-Loire et martyr à La Réole en 1004*. Paris, 1872.

Pfister, Christian. *Études sur la règne de Robert le Pieux*. Paris, 1885.

Picavet, François. *Gerbert, un Pape philosophe*. Paris, 1897.

Poole, Reginald L. *Illustrations of the History of Mediaeval Thought and Learning*. New York, 1920.

Rijk, L.M. de. "On the Curriculum of the Arts of the Trivium at St. Gall from c.850-c.1000," *Vivarium* I (1963), 35-86.

Robinson, J. Armitage. *The Times of St. Dunstan*. Oxford, 1923.

Rocher, Charles. *Histoire de l'abbaye royale de Saint-Benoît-sur-Loire*. Orleans, 1865.

Sackur, Ernst. *Die Cluniacenser*. Halle, 1892.

Schmitz, Philibert. *Histoire de l'Ordre de Saint-Benoît* vol. II. Maredsous, 1942.

Schramm, Percy E. *Kaiser, Rom und Renovatio*. Leipzig, 1929.

Schrörs, H. "Erzbischof Bruno von Köln, einer geschliche Charakteristik," *Annalen des historischer Vereins für dem Niederrhein* C (1911), 1-92.

Sievers, Bernard, "Der heilige Bernward von Hildesheim als Bischof Künstler and Sohn des heiligen Benedict, *"Studien und Mitteilungen aus den Benedictiner und Cistercienser Orden* XIV (1893), 398-420;589-627.

Singer, Charles and Dorothea. "Byrhtferth's Diagram," *Bodleian Quarterly Review* II (1917), 47-51.

Sisam, Kenneth. *Studies in the History of Old English Literature.* Oxford, 1953.

Specht, Franz. *Geschichte der Unterreichswesen in Deutschland.* Stuttgart, 1885.

Stammler, Wolfgang and Langosch, Karl. *Die deutsche Literatur des Mittelalters.* Berlin, 1955.

Stenton, Frank M. *Anglo-Saxon England.* Oxford, 1943.

Taylor, Henry O. *The Mediaeval Mind.* London, 1938.

Thompson, James W. "The Introduction of Arabic Science into Lorraine in the Tenth Century," *Isis* XII (1929), 184-195.

____ *The Medieval Library.* Chicago, 1939.

Tschan, Francis J. *Saint Bernward of Hildesheim: His Life and Times.* Notre Dame, 1942-52.

Tupper, Frederick, Jr. "History and Texts of the Benedictine Reform of the Tenth Century," *Modern Language Notes* VIII (1893), 314-367.

Van de Vyver, A. "Les premières traductions latines de traités arabes sur l'astrolabe," *Mémoires du Ier Congrès international de Géographie historique* II (1931), 206-290.

Waddell, Helen. *The Wandering Scholars.* 7th ed. London, 1966.

Warichez, Joseph. *L'Abbaye de Lobbes.* Louvain, 1909.

White, Caroline L. *Aelfric: A New Study of his Life and Writings.* Yale Studies in English II. New Haven, 1898; reprint Hamden, Connecticut, 1974.

White, Lynn, et. al. "Symposium on the Tenth Century," *Medievalia et Humanistica* IX (1955), 3-29.

Wormald, Francis. *The Benedictional of St. Ethelwold.* London, 1959.

Zinner, Ernst. "Gerbert und das Sehrohr," *Bericht der Naturforschunde Gesellschaft Bamberg* XXXII (1952),39-40.

Zumthor, Paul. *Histoire littéraire de la France médiévale VIe - XIVe siècles.* Paris, 1954.

Index